BRITISH
POSTERS

First published by V&A Publishing, 2012
Victoria and Albert Museum
South Kensington
London SW7 2RL
www.vandabooks.com

Distributed in North America by Harry N. Abrams Inc., New York

Paperback edition
ISBN 9781 85177 676 4

Library of Congress Control Number 2011935132

10 9 8 7 6 5 4 3 2 1
2016 2015 2014 2013 2012

Designer: Will Webb
Copy-editor: Liz Cowen
Indexer: Hilary Bird

V&A Photography by V&A Photographic Studio and the Factory Project

Printed in Hong Kong

BRITISH POSTERS
ADVERTISING, ART & ACTIVISM
CATHERINE FLOOD

V&A PUBLISHING

Contents

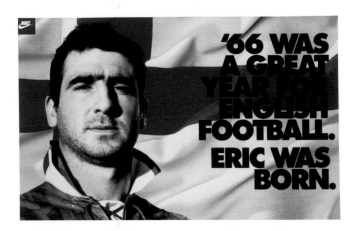

Foreword

The changing role of the poster during the past 70 years is a stimulating subject for debate. How has it adapted to new means of communication and shifts in artistic practice? Does it retain its command as an effective tool of advertising, as a powerful instrument of propaganda, as an exciting and influential design form? Catherine Flood traces new directions, both mainstream and alternative, for the poster during the post-war period and into a digital age. As well as examining design developments, she also engages with the poster in the contexts of its environment and of public response, seeking out many fresh sources to offer a fascinating and original perspective. Although much has been written about the posters in the Victoria and Albert Museum (whose national collection is summarized below), this is the first time that its post-war holdings have been explored in a rounded survey.

The V&A has actively collected posters for over a century, recognizing their importance within the history of graphic design. They were chosen as exemplars of artistic style, form and technique, reflecting the major developments in poster design from the late nineteenth century (when an expansion of mass advertising first combined with key developments in colour lithography to attract artists to experiment in the medium) to the present day. Acquisitions reflect stylistic movements such as Art Nouveau, Art Deco, Modernism, Surrealism, Pop, Psychedelia and Street Art. While the collection is decidedly international, there is particular strength in its British representation, often as the result of generous gifts.

The poster's inherent qualities – a popular and ubiquitous appeal and an ability to communicate messages in compelling visual shorthand – have made it a magnet for advertiser, designer and consumer alike. The Museum's collections offer an insight into changing artistic practice in commercial advertising. From early hoarding-size posters for Bovril, Colman's Mustard and Guinness, to more recent campaigns for Benson & Hedges, Nike and the Wonderbra, the use of branding, advertising strategies and marketing devices can be explored. So too can the role of the patron. During its inter-war heyday, poster art flourished under the enlightened patronage of companies such as London Underground, the railway companies, Shell-Mex and the General Post Office, all of which judged good design to be a prestigious and effective means of reaching their target audience.

The collections also reflect the dawn of the 'New Advertising' or 'Creative Revolution' in the 1950s and 1960s, and the rise of advertising agencies' creative teams and graphic design groups. However, as this book illustrates, the role of the commercial poster now is once more changing radically, in line with new technologies and the realities of instant global communication. At the same time, in the contemporary and graphic art scene, the poster has found fertile new territory in projects such as the Art on the Underground installations, in limited-edition commissions and in self-publishing enterprises.

Plate 1
KEEP BRITAIN TIDY
Tom Eckersley, produced by the
Central Office of Information
for the Ministry of Housing and
Social Government, 1962–3
Offset lithograph in black,
red and blue
V&A: 501–1985

Plate 2
COME ON PILGRIM
Vaughan Oliver, photograph by
Simon Larbalestier. Published
for 4AD promoting an album by
the rock band The Pixies, c.1987
Offset lithograph
V&A: E.326–1989

While the V&A has always been concerned with the graphic design and techniques of posters, it has also recognized their value as historic evidence. Political issues and unique events (two world wars, the Russian Revolution, the Spanish Civil War, general elections) prompted acquisitions which reveal the poster's potential as an instrument of mass communication and catalyst for change. That the poster can also offer an inexpensive, focused and often low-tech means of generating publicity is illustrated by early women's suffrage block prints, May 1968 student protest screen-prints, and late twentieth-century community campaigns. Stirring examples of counter-culture propaganda from the 1960s and '70s featured in the gift of the Schreyer Collection in 2002, while pro-democracy movements in Central and Eastern Europe in 1989–90 triggered on-the-spot collection by the Museum. These are now joined by hard-hitting graphics generated by recent political debates such as the anti-Iraq War protests.

The V&A's posters can be searched online, and viewed in the Prints and Drawings Study Room. In 1998, *The Power of the Poster* brought the full range of the collections to a new audience, while more recent shows, such as *Art Deco* (2003), *Modernism* (2006), *Cold War Modern* (2008) and *A Century of Olympic Posters* (2008), all accompanied by publications, have featured specific aspects of the collection.

Margaret Timmers

Introduction

The poster is a form that excites extraordinary interest. Posters have a fleeting life span, but a propensity to be remembered and preserved that sets them apart from other forms of printed ephemera. They litter both our everyday lives and collective cultural memory. This book maps how the poster has developed in Britain since the Second World War in the hands of graphic designers, advertising agencies, counter-cultural groups and fine artists. It is the story of a traditional medium adapting within an increasingly complex terrain of advertising and communication, and it covers a period of profound change in how posters are produced, used and encountered. Despite frequent predictions of its demise, the poster has remained an irresistible proposition for a variety of practitioners, even in a digital age of social networking and viral communication.

The poster's unique status as an object of art and design can be traced back to its beginnings in the late nineteenth-century city, where it emerged as a means of harnessing the consumer power of the growing urban crowd. Large full-colour posters composed of pictures as well as words were made possible by advances in the printing process of colour lithography and introduced a sensational flood of images onto the street. The public interest they aroused intensified when a number of Paris-based avant-garde artists turned their hands to the medium in the 1890s (the most famous was Henri de Toulouse-Lautrec). The poster was hailed as a new and modern art form and therefore something to understand and possess. Like the butterflies they

Plate 3
L'OREAL PARIS, BECAUSE YOU'RE WORTH IT
Stephen Gill, photograph from the Billboards series, 1999–2003
C-type print
V&A: E.203–2005

Plate 4
ST WAYNE
Billboard by Wieden Kennedy
for Nike, London, 2006

were said to resemble, posters became objects not just to admire in their natural outdoor habitat, but to capture, collect and catalogue. A brief and international frenzy for poster collecting laid the foundations for a historiography of the poster and a canon of poster art. Graphic design has since extended into all areas of visual communication, but posters continued to be singled out, exhibited and written about. This is still true today, perhaps most noticeably in a number of international biennales and festivals that celebrate contemporary poster design. For designers the lure of the poster lies in this great weight of tradition and in the freedom it presents to indulge in scale and form: 'a rectangular arena in which to exercise their most expressive, experimental and potentially significant work'.[1]

Fascination with the poster ranges beyond the realms of art and design. Their time-specific, fugitive nature gives posters meaning and poignancy as historical documents. Anchored to the life-cycles of products or calendars of events and entertainments, posters are usually current and on display for a few short weeks before they are torn down and replaced. On the street they are the constantly refreshed contemporary face of the city – its living skin. Occasionally this process of destruction and renewal is arrested. In 2010 modernization work at Notting Hill Gate Underground station uncovered a complete wall of posters left in situ when a passageway was sealed off in 1959 (plate 5). The discovery of the posters provided an immediate sense of temporality, turning a disused passage into an outsize time capsule. Like a datable layer of archaeology, they offer a glimpse of the city at a particular moment and place – evidence of what Londoners in 1959 saw and were prompted to think about as they went about their daily journeys. By directing our gaze and imagination, posters help define our visual experience of urban space, determining both what we see and what we do not see (plate 3). Posters flesh out many different kinds of history. In Britain they have been acquired by museums and archives, university libraries and private collections, where they preserve the heritage of particular institutions or illuminate subjects of war, transport, public health and so on. Another reason for posters' cultural prominence is undoubtedly the fact that they

Plate 5
Posters dating from *c*.1959
uncovered at Notting Hill Gate
Underground station, 2010

make compelling illustrations. Designs created to be eye-catching at a distance can be successfully scaled down and transposed to the page or computer screen. Some posters achieve a prolific afterlife through this kind of replication; a few hit a cultural nerve and become iconic, defining images of the events they outlive.

In addressing the subject of British posters, the emphasis of this survey lies less in teasing out native trends in art and design than in identifying how the poster as a medium has developed in relation to socio-economic, political and cultural life in Britain. Included in this approach is the idea of Britain as a physical, architectural context for poster display. The starting point is the period of post-war reconstruction. After the Second World War there was a new faith in planning and design and high hopes for the role the poster might play in the project of rebuilding Britain. It was also a point when the practice of poster design was on the cusp of change. Graphic design was beginning to emerge as a professional discipline based on the technical specification of word and image and would start to sideline the painterly freelance poster designer who had presided over a golden age of prestige poster advertising in Britain between the wars. Chapter 1 follows the poster through the evolving structures of mainstream graphic design and advertising in Britain up to the end of the twentieth century. The focus here is on the poster as it is traditionally defined – a large sheet of printed paper, displayed in a public place for the purpose of delivering information, advertising or propaganda and where the design is typically the result of a commercial relationship between creative professionals and a client with a brief.

Plate 6
ANTI (ART) FAIR
John Maybury, with a self-
portrait by Trojan and computer
text by Leslie Weiner, 1986
Colour screenprint
V&A: E. 310–2011

Chapter 2 retraces the same period, looking at alternative contexts in which poster production flourished. In the milieux of youth culture and counter-culture that developed in post-war Britain, posters, like dress, provided an affordable (sometimes DIY) means of attaining visibility and intervening in an environment. These are posters 'that always carried the subtext "we are here"'.[2] In the 1960s Pop Art and a fast-paced youth market gave a new currency to the mass-produced, throw-away form of the poster: the poster proved itself to be an ideal vehicle for turning the imagery appropriated by pop culture into a simple form of merchandise and wall art for the home. Eventually this process of domestication led to a second dictionary definition of the poster as 'a large printed picture (which may or may not be an advertisement) suitable for decorative display'.[3] Artists seeking fresh ways of working were attracted by the ephemeral and public condition of the poster while for protest groups it was a low-tech way in which to challenge the sophisticated machine of the mainstream media. Compared with the posters described in Chapter 1, much of this material is the result of a more personal relationship between the designer and the message or movement espoused in the poster. This division of material also acknowledges differences in the technical resources available and in the modes of distribution and display.

Chapter 3 considers the poster in the early twenty-first century when digital media are transforming the dynamics of time, space and cost in all contexts of contemporary communication: from multi-national advertising, to general elections, to student activism. At this point the story of the poster becomes an interplay between the virtual and the real; between pixels on a screen and print on paper; between the seemingly limitless scope of cyberspace and the ever more tightly regulated space of the physical city.

POST-WAR RECONSTRUCTION

In 1945 the war was won. 'And Now –' exhorted a Labour Party election poster 'Win the Peace' (plate 7). As Britain looked to the challenges and possibilities of post-war reconstruction, poster designers had a sense of idealism about their medium and what it could contribute to the task. 'Britain and her industries', declared the magazine *Art and Industry* in 1948, 'have in their poster designers a valuable force which can make a large contribution to British revival'.[1] The commercial function of posters in lubricating the economy, however, was problematic while rationing continued and industrial output was directed at export markets. The government urged advertisers to limit their activities to avoid increasing inflationary demand for scarce goods. It was in the social and political project of reshaping Britain that poster designers felt there was scope for their work. The experience of 'total war' had encouraged people to question what vision of Britain they were fighting for, and in the early 1940s a commitment had emerged to planning a fairer post-war society (plate 8). This was to involve the poster in terms of new approaches to public information and public space.

The government's successful use of posters during the war suggested a new peacetime mission for the poster in communicating collective social goals. In 1948 Abram Games, one of Britain's foremost exponents of the poster, wrote that poster designers 'are anxious that the lessons of their unique contribution in war should not be forgotten but developed in the interests of the whole community and serve the greater cause of peace'.[2] Apart from the gentlemanly campaigns of the Empire Marketing Board, inter-war British governments had not considered persuasive publicity a legitimate activity for the state. The propaganda poster was tarnished by the militarism of the Great War and was closely associated with totalitarian regimes in Germany, Italy and the Soviet Union. During the Second World War (the 'people's war'), however, poster designers helped the Ministry of Information to develop a more egalitarian tone of address in its propaganda, in line with a popular shift towards social

Plate 7
**AND NOW – WIN THE PEACE.
VOTE LABOUR**
Unknown designer for
the Labour Party, 1945
Colour lithograph

Plate 8
**YOUR BRITAIN,
FIGHT FOR IT NOW**
Abram Games, issued by the
Army Bureau of Current Affairs,
1942
Colour lithograph
V&A: E.1886–2004

One of a series of three
posters designed to help
people imagine how Britain
could change for the better in
a post-war future. A block of
workers' flats built in a modern
architectural style replaces
crumbling slums.

democracy. By balancing themes of collective sacrifice and citizenship with increased state responsibility for informing and protecting the people, war posters had set out a form of social contract between the government and the British people. The landslide Labour victory in 1945 and the creation of the Welfare State consolidated the public-interest poster as a voice of expanded and socially engaged government in Britain. The Central Office of Information (COI) was established to take on the mantle of the wartime Ministry of Information, indicating that communication would remain a government priority. In 1948 the COI was using an enormous one-fifth of all available outdoor advertising space, with campaigns targeting production, fuel economy and health and safety.

Posters gave government welfare policy visibility on the street, where they could be received either as evidence of a government taking action and exercising a duty of care, or as an unwelcome intervention by the state into people's lines of sight and daily lives. One early post-war road safety poster dubbed the 'Black Widow' produced a particularly strong public reaction, which was expressed in letters to newspapers and questions in parliament, but most of all by graffiti over copies of the poster itself (plate 9). A Mass Observation survey recorded that 58 per cent of examples examined on display in London had been defaced.[3] People found coming face to face with the poster shocking and depressing, seeing a raw reminder of wartime deaths in the portrait of the widow and a dour emblem of 'austerity Britain' in her chalky, washed-out appearance. Much of the graffiti involved 'cheering her up' with additions of lipstick, rouge and eyeliner. The 'Black Widow''s unflatteringly bare face on a public poster was deemed unpalatable – unpatriotic and defeatist even. The

expected role of poster displays and of the female image in particular was to provide
colour and glamour in the environment.

As one Mass Observation respondent remarked, the poster was 'something
out of the ordinary'. During the war, poster designers had tended to avoid emotional
appeals and images of distress, adopting either humour or a rational juxtaposition of
ideas in 'a skilful composition of elements leading to logical conclusions' – a style
exemplified by Tom Eckersley's posters for the Royal Society for the Prevention of
Accidents (plate 10).[4] The 'Black Widow', however, relied on shock tactics, a more
coercive form of persuasion. It was felt to be too heavy-handed, especially at a
moment when the relationship of state and society was being redrawn. People

resisted either by obliterating the image or answering back, and writing on the poster became a popular means of commenting on the government. Across the country people added the caption 'She Voted Labour'. Although in another instance someone gave the widow the tag line 'Mine's a Miner' – an expression of support perhaps for the imminent nationalization of the notoriously dangerous coal industry, which many welcomed as a humanitarian step.[5]

A very different social poster project was the 'Map Review' series produced by the Bureau of Current Affairs (BCA). The BCA was set up as an independent organization in 1946 to continue the adult education work of the Army Bureau of Current Affairs in a civilian context. Its mission was to pave the way for social development by creating an 'informed, alert and critical public opinion', and it aimed to

Plate 10
A CHILD'S LIFE MAY DEPEND ON YOUR BRAKES
Tom Eckersley, issued by the Royal Society for the Prevention of Accidents, 1948
Colour lithograph
V&A: E.871–2004

As people started to drive again after the war, road safety became an urgent public concern. Cars had not been maintained, drivers were out of practice and a new generation of children were unused to busy roads.

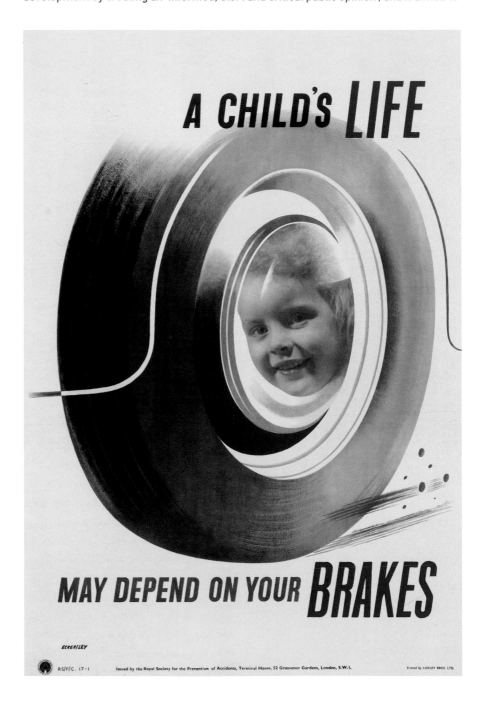

Plate 11

**WORK AND PLAY FOR THE
SIXTEEN TO TWENTIES**

Unknown designer, issued by
the Bureau of Current Affairs,
1948 as part of the 'Map Review'
series
Colour lithograph
V&A: E.124–1994

achieve this by publishing a programme of materials to support co-operative current affairs discussion groups. 'Map Review' was a visual aid issued fortnightly on a particular topic of British life or international politics, plotting out the subject through diagrams, photographs and short texts (plate 11). Copies were distributed to secondary schools, social services, church groups, libraries, factories and the army. They could be used as wall charts or spread across a table for people to group around. It was the poster format used as information design and a focal point for collective discussion rather than direct persuasion – although there was often felt to be a guiding left-wing bias in the content. The BCA publishing experiment exemplified the practical social idealism that flourished immediately after the war. It closed in 1951 when an initial grant from the Carnegie Trust, a charitable foundation, ran out, by which time the political climate in Britain had shifted to the right with the election of a Conservative government.

While the government and the BCA both used posters to pursue ideals of reconstruction, themes of recovery permeated posters that had no direct propaganda agenda. In some cases the geographies of reconstruction and post-war land planning are evident in the transport posters of the period and the way in which they presented the British landscape. Between the wars posters issued by railway companies, London Transport and petrol providers (Shell in particular), encouraging people to travel out of town, had helped to foster an idea of the British countryside as a site of collective heritage and recreation. This romantic but democratic idea of the land gained institutional currency after the war with the creation of national parks, Green Belt policy and the expansion of the National Trust, but was offset by the urgent need to increase agricultural production and drive forward the mechanization of farming. A series of posters, 'Out & About', produced by the newly nationalized London Transport in 1949–50 reflected these dual concerns with preservation and progress in relation to the land. Two of the posters in the series, 'Country Churches' and 'Country Houses', dealt with the countryside as an historical artefact . 'The Streams' is a detailed illustration of a natural habitat, picking up on a new wave of naturalism based on ecology and the observant citizen-scientist. 'The Farms' meanwhile presents a scene alive with human activity (plates 12a and 12b). Tractors and stockbreeding, two king-

Plates 12a and b
THE FARMS. OUT & ABOUT BY LONDON TRANSPORT
James Arnold, issued by London Transport, 1950
Colour lithograph
V&A: E.694–1950 and
E.694.a–1950

Pair posters were a format that London Transport introduced in the 1940s. One half presented the main image, leaving the other half free for words. They were designed for the captive audience on station platforms, who had time to absorb involved images and read lengthy texts.

pins in the modernization of farming, have a prominent place in the composition. The accompanying text instructs the Londoner to take pleasure in the practical use of farmland as well as in its scenic beauty.

Poster production after the war was beset by shortages of materials and a depleted print industry, but the post-war cityscape provided new spaces for posters, which spread over the surfaces of derelict buildings and followed hardy weeds into areas of bomb damage, colonizing the fences erected to shield bombsites. In cities that had endured bombings and blackouts for six years and were now ground down by economic crisis, poster displays could offer visual respite. In 1948 James Fitton (himself a poster designer) painted a scene in Brixton where a boarded-up shop front had been covered in posters, describing it 'blooming like a flower in such a drab setting' (plate 13).[6] Others, however, viewed the situation as anarchic and unseemly. The *New Statesman* complained that 'Blitzed London might have had a sad dignity of its own, but it is disappearing behind a galloping rash of advertising posters.'[7] The

gaps that bombs had left in cities encouraged the use of massive 64-sheet posters (304.8 x 912.9cm), contributing to a feeling that posters were getting out of hand (plate 14). In this sense they symbolized the dual planning challenges of 'blitz and blight'.

Since the late nineteenth century there had been a vocal lobby in Britain (headed by the Council for the Protection of Rural England) determined to resist outdoor advertising on the grounds that it despoiled the countryside and damaged the civic dignity of towns; a stance informed, among other things, by an intellectual distaste for commerce. Advertisers had consequently exercised a degree of self-regulation in order to maintain public goodwill and stave off regulation by parliament. After the Second World War these long-standing concerns with the poster as an eyesore converged with the mandate of the Labour government to radically overhaul the control of land use, with the result that outdoor advertising was comprehensively regulated for the first time under the 1947 Town and Country Planning Act. Coming into effect in July 1948, the Act established a legislative framework for the British poster, granting local authorities power over the placement of outdoor advertising, which could no longer be agreed between landowner and advertiser without reference to the state. Arguments over outdoor advertising went to the heart of contemporary debates over who controlled and benefited from public space and touched on the grand themes of state control and nationalization versus commercial market freedom. On the one hand 'the galloping rash of advertising posters' was a symptom of the 'chaos of economic do-as-they-please anarchy' rejected in the Labour Party's 1945 manifesto and an 'abuse of private rights at the expense of the community'[8] (although the government itself was an offender when it came to poster display). On the other, restrictions on poster advertising were held up as evidence that 'the era of organised dreariness has indeed encroached even farther on our traditional freedoms than we thought'.[9] The regulations controlling advertising enshrined in the 1947 Act remain substantially unchanged today: a testimony both to their comprehensiveness and the degree to which their application has channelled our sensibilities regarding outdoor advertising.

Plate 14
Bert Hardy, photograph
originally published in *Picture
Post*, 1949. It shows a game
of cricket being played on
a London bombsite. The
enormous billboard was part
of a government campaign to
impress on people the gravity
of the economic situation
in Britain and encourage
increased productivity.

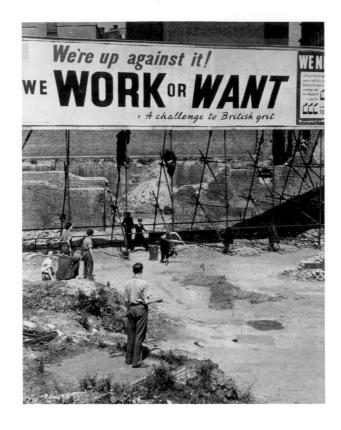

An early high-profile challenge under the new Act was directed against the billboards in Trafalgar Square in 1952–3. Trafalgar Square was a location of spectacles – of tourism, public pageants, community gatherings and political demonstrations – and the proposed banishment of advertising posters from the square's mix of urban display and messaging was a significant statement. A press report of the case stated that the removal of advertisements would designate Trafalgar Square a 'national place'. The square was described as somewhere 'where there had been an accumulation of historic associations and traditions' and that advertisements were 'incongruous and out of harmony' with these traditions.[10]

At the same time the architect and designer Sir Hugh Casson was engaged in planning a scheme of street decorations along the route of Queen Elizabeth II's coronation procession, which was to pass through Trafalgar Square. He factored in the 'conspicuous' impact of advertising hoardings along the route and asked advertisers to produce topical posters for the occasion in which their product was subsidiary to a loyal message so that the commercial pitch of the advertiser did not detract from the patriotic milieu of the streets.[11] Guinness occupied one of the contested billboards in Trafalgar Square, which were still in place during the coronation and it was easy for them to oblige: their distinctive posters by John Gilroy were so familiar that no advertising copy was required for the public to instantly identify their coronation offering with the 'Guinness for Strength' campaign. On the poster the Guinness brand characters are depicted being lifted above the heads of the crowd, while in Trafalgar Square the poster itself soared over the procession (plates 15 and 16). The episode illustrates a degree of friction regarding outdoor advertising flowing both from the idea of the modern planned city and the resurgent themes of national heritage that infused the coronation.

Plate 15 (right)
John Gilroy, produced by S. H.
Benson for Arthur Guinness Son
& Co. Ltd, 1953
Colour lithograph
V&A: E.154–1973

A version of this poster designed
to tie in with the coronation
of Queen Elizabeth II was
displayed on a large billboard in
Trafalgar Square with the text
'Loyal Greetings'. It features the
menagerie of animals associated
with the Guinness brand and
belongs to the 'Guinness for
Strength' campaign, which
had been running since the
early 1930s.

Plate 16 (below)
A Guinness poster occupying a
prominent position in Trafalgar
Square as the coronation
procession of Queen Elizabeth II
passes by on 2 June 1953.

COMMERCIAL ART, GRAPHIC DESIGN AND THE 'CREATIVE REVOLUTION'

The ideals surrounding the poster immediately after the war, both as a designed object and as an element in the architectural environment, reflected a new faith placed in design and planning as part of the reconstruction effort. Design was enshrined in public policy – through initiatives such as the creation of the Council of Industrial Design in 1944 and the formalization of design education. Over the next 20 years, as Britain moved from austerity to economic boom, this process of professionalization continued to roll forward. The growth of the design and advertising industries in Britain ushered in new approaches and new business models. These factors, together with advances in technology and an increasing openness to international styles, affected how posters were produced and what they looked like.

Visual design in Britain in the late 1940s and '50s reflected an insular mood; a retreat into an idea of Britishness after the trauma of the war. Ealing films mythologized a charming old England of potty aristocrats, eccentric local communities and branch-line railways, while the posters that promoted them delved into British traditions of canal-boat folk art, brass rubbings and fairground lettering (plate 17). The 'Contemporary Style' that prevailed after the Festival of Britain in 1951 was a softened version of European modernism, mixing graphic simplification and abstraction with decorative vernacular elements and revived eighteenth- and nineteenth-century typefaces: nostalgia for the past projected into a modernist future. Abram Games's emblem for the Festival of Britain is a good example: a bold contemporary motif lightened by a jaunty swag of bunting (plate 18). Peacetime advertising was distinguished from war posters by a more illustrative and often whimsical touch. By the early 1960s, however, a new generation of designers were starting to

Plate 17
PAINTED BOATS
John Piper for Ealing Studios, 1945
Colour lithograph
V&A: Circ.339–1971

The film *Painted Boats* was a documentary-style story about life on the English canals.

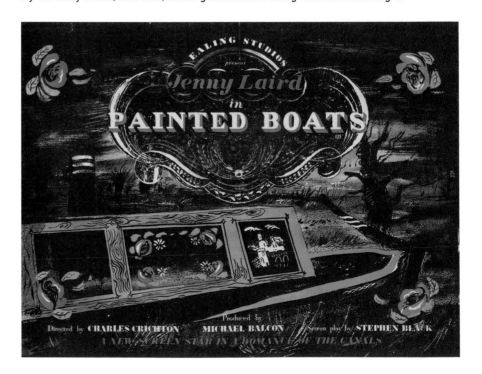

Plate 18
**FESTIVAL OF BRITAIN,
MAY 3–SEPTEMBER 30**
Unknown designer, published
by the Festival of Britain
Colour lithograph, 1951
V&A: E.308-2011

Plate 19
**MEN WHO MEAN BUSINESS
READ THE FINANCIAL TIMES
EVERY DAY**
Abram Games for the
Financial Times, 1951
Colour Lithograph
V&A: E.156-1980

synthesize international influences, looking to the rigours of Swiss typographic design and the verve of American advertising.

In parallel with developments in style, visual communication was extending its reach in Britain through new technologies and services with profound effects on how design and advertising were practised. In the 1930s poster design was the apex of the craft-based field of 'commercial art'. The majority of poster work originated in the studios of advertising agencies and printers, but the most prestigious commissions went to a handful of freelance poster designers and fine artists. A top tier of poster design was supported by the patronage of a number of institutions (Shell-Mex, the railway companies, the Empire Marketing Board and the General Post Office), led by the example of London Transport, who applied principles of design reform to their advertising and allowed the artists and designers they commissioned considerable creative freedom.

Of the important designers of the 1950s, however, only Abram Games and Tom Eckersley continued to define themselves as poster specialists in this tradition. Their contemporaries F.H.K. Henrion and Hans Schleger (pseudonym Zero) both set up design studios which undertook a more diverse diet of work including exhibition design and house styles. It was becoming less realistic and satisfying for a designer to

Plate 20
**THOUSANDS OF JOBS ARE
FILLED BY THE EMPLOYMENT
EXCHANGES EVERY DAY**
Reginald Mount and Eileen
Evans, produced by the Central
Office of Information for the
Ministry of Labour, c.1964
Offset lithograph in black, red
and orange
V&A: E.459–1995

survive chiefly through poster commissions. The advent of commercial television in 1955 had a huge impact by siphoning advertising budgets and creative energy away from the poster, while the colour supplements in Sunday newspapers that appeared during the 1960s provided a lavish new platform for press advertising. The rise of the supermarket was a further factor, focusing attention on packaging and shop design as an immediate method of attracting customers. Prestige poster advertising had been at the cutting edge of visual culture in the 1930s, but this was no longer the case. While the poster designer retained a definite aura, he was, as fellow graphic designer David Gentleman has put it, 'a big fish in a rapidly shrinking pond'.[12]

Abram Games was the consummate dextrous graphic author who could execute his signature with an airbrush. The metamorphosis of commercial art into what came to be recognized as graphic design implied a move away from this model of the designer as 'one man and his crayon or airbrush'.[13] Typographer and design historian Paul Stiff described how the post-war visual environment in Britain continued to look 'airbrushed, hog's hair hand-lettered, chalked, penned and washed . . . '[14] But as designers took over the control of typography from printers, and photography became an increasingly important component in visual communication, their task evolved from autographic image-making to one of technical specification within an industrial process: the urgent demands of communication during the war had accelerated the use of photomechanical printing processes.

Group practice became the norm for designers in the 1960s, enabling them to meet the demands of Britain's economic boom and take on larger commercial jobs, while retaining more independence than was possible working for an advertising agency. Several companies were founded during this period that were to reshape the design industry in Britain. These included BDMW (Derek Birdsall, George Daulby, George Mayhew and Peter Wildbur), Fletcher, Forbes, Gill (Alan Fletcher, Colin Forbes and Bob Gill) which later became Pentagram, Minale Tattersfield (Marcello Minale and Brian Tattersfield) and Main Wolff – later Wolff Olins (designers of the London 2012 Olympic Games logo). The topography of ad-land in Britain was also changing, with the appearance on the scene of adventurous new agencies such as Collett Dickenson Pearce (which became one of Britain's most successful agencies and a nursery for advertising talents) and American firms such as Doyle Dane Bernbach opening London offices. The founding of British Design and Art Direction (D&AD) and its annual awards was heralded by many as a forum for a confident new wave of design and advertising in Britain.

Many from this new generation of professionals embraced the 'big idea' approach of American advertising: a defining aspect of the changes in method on Madison Avenue which came to be described as the 'creative revolution'. Under this rubric, the concept was all important and the designer's hand was subordinated to his (and occasionally her) flash of inspiration and wit. In graphic design, this was manifested in the adoption of a problem-solving approach. Tom Eckersley's 1954 guide to poster design had exhorted aspiring freelance poster designers to develop a unique personal style.[15] *Graphic Design: Visual Comparisons*, published just under a decade later in 1963 by Fletcher, Forbes, Gill, by contrast set out what was to become a familiar thesis: 'that any one visual problem has an infinite number of solutions; that many of them are valid; that solutions ought to derive from the subject matter; that the designer should therefore have no preconceived graphic style'.[16]

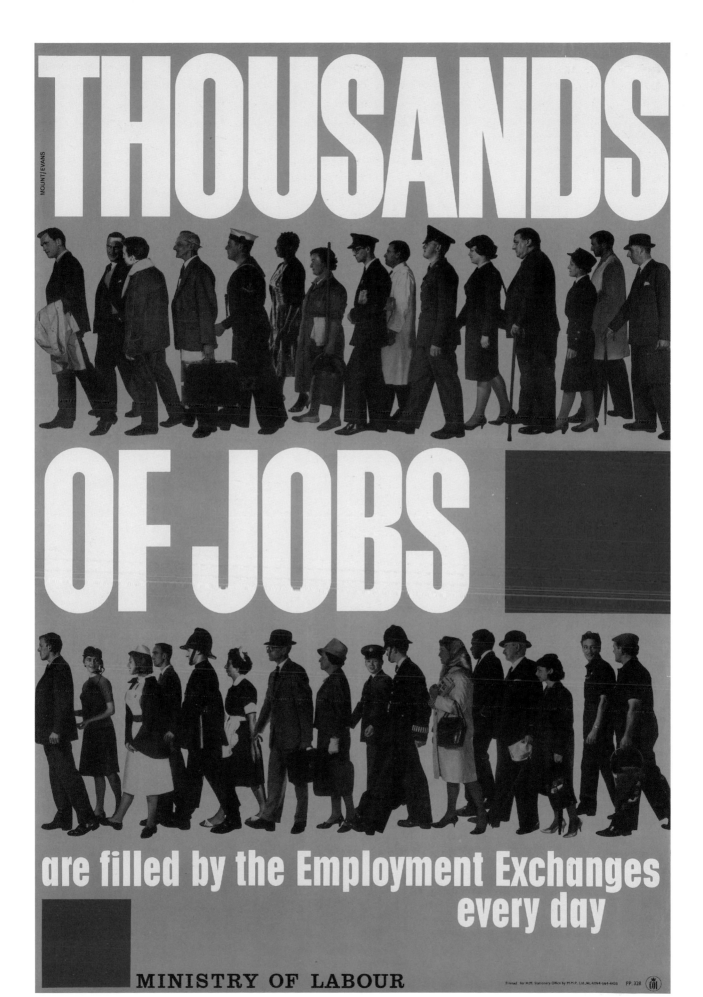

Another important change in approach to poster design was an increasing use of photography. In the 1940s and '50s, elements of black-and-white photography were frequently incorporated into poster designs to introduce visual contrast or an element of authenticity. By the 1960s advances in colour photography and printing and reliable flash-lighting meant that an advertising poster could rely on a single image composed through the camera lens. A new profession of advertising photographers emerged whose job was to realize an art director's idea, 'to soak up the essence of a good brief and set about bringing it to life'.[17] The most famous were Terence Donovan, Brian Duffy and David Bailey. As the advertising industry entered a golden age of fabulous production budgets and epic location shoots the visual focus was on the immediate, realistic images delivered by photographers and television cameramen.

Plate 21
GO TO WORK ON AN EGG
Mather & Crowther (art director: Ruth Gill; photographer: Len Fulford; copywriters: Fay Weldon and Mary Gowing). Produced for the British Egg Marketing Board, *c.*1964 Colour offset lithograph V&A: E.309–2011

The marker-pen-style illustration of the girl on top of the egg gives the impression of a witty idea quickly scribbled down by the designer.

Plate 22
ADD AN EGG – ADD GOODNESS
Unknown designer, issued
by the British Egg Marketing
Board, c.1965
Colour offset lithograph
V&A: E.552–1985

This poster relies on still-life
photography and good colour
printing to deliver an enticingly
real presentation of the subject.

Add an egg –add goodness

Consequently there was a feeling that the British tradition of poster design established between the wars was being lost. In 1962 the Society of Industrial Artists and the Council of Industrial Design (which both now represented something of an old guard) set up an annual poster competition intended to inspire interest in poster design. Year by year it turned out to be an exercise in disappointment as judges and commentators looked for qualities that were no longer commercially relevant. A recurring complaint was that graphic talent was being replaced by the work of copywriters and photographers: 'the poster industry is . . . inclined to feast on its own cleverness, putting too much reliance on the non-visual art of the copywriter, or the rather mindless fecundity of the camera'.[18] With the poster often relegated to a supporting role in advertising strategy, reminding people of a message they had already encountered on television or in a magazine, there were accusations that posters were becoming nothing more than enlarged press ads or TV stills. Certainly advertising agencies approached their task in terms of thinking up an advertisement and getting the right shot, rather than creating a poster with its own dynamics of scale and display. Some of the most imaginative posters of the period, however, fully exploited the site-specific quality of their medium: Fletcher, Forbes, Gill did a bus-side poster for Pirelli slippers in which the passengers sitting on the bus complete the image like a game of 'misfits' (plate 23).

Plate 23
Fletcher, Forbes, Gill,
bus-side poster advertising
Pirelli slippers, 1961

By the beginning of the 1960s outdoor poster advertising was held to be in decline. Billboard space had been reduced under the provisions of the Town and Country Planning Act and an exodus of advertising to television meant remaining billboards sometimes stayed blank and dormant. During this period, the intensification of the Cold War provided an ideological defence of outdoor advertising, which could be valued as a spectacular manifestation of capitalism: part of the dressing of Western cities that differentiated them from communist ones. Advertising's physical presence seemed to confirm the citizen-consumer's freedom of choice in the market and by extension at the ballot box. An attack on advertising at this period could be construed as an attack on a way of life. In an extraordinary statement of propaganda, billboard companies in 1958 were filling their empty sites with the message: 'Advertising introduces you to the good things of life and has done much to create your high standard of living'.[19] In an article in *The Times* in 1961 warning local authorities in Britain not to be over-zealous in restricting poster hoardings, British politician Lord Boothby rehearsed a popular vision of gloomy cities behind the Iron Curtain and the 'the effect of drabness and lack of colour on the lives of the people'. 'Suddenly,' he writes, 'the root cause of the trouble dawned on me in a blinding flash of discernment. It was the total absence of outdoor advertising.'[20] In reality, by the early 1960s, Boothby's view was becoming harder to support as opposition to advertising in the post-Stalinist Eastern Bloc began to thaw: in Warsaw a flowering of neon signs on city buildings had begun in the late 1950s.[21]

Gordon Cullen's theory of Townscape (published in 1961 in *Concise Townscape*) outlined an approach to town planning that was to an extent sympathetic with the visual variety created by outdoor advertising. In promoting a form of urban design that was more human and organic than the anodyne geometry of post-war town planning (the 'three-dimensional diagram in which people are asked to live'), Cullen argued that outdoor advertising was a fact of modern city life ('People still like to buy and sell, to proclaim and to notice') and one that planners should embrace for the lively and surreal incongruities and textures it creates.[22] Cullen savoured the contrasts of scale that outdoor advertising could produce – comparing the impact of a billboard to the shock of coming across the Cerne Abbas giant (an ancient chalk carving) in the Dorset hills. The parlance of local authorities applying planning regulations on the ground, however, was more likely to be about 'making the poster fit the town' through a harmonious integration of advertising into the architectural scene.[23]

Local authorities interpreted the advertising regulations within the Town and Country Planning Act to enable them to clear poster sites from rural and residential areas. Billboard companies retrenched by focusing their energies on more select and valuable sites, in terms of the volume, profile and the likely mindset of people passing by. Favoured positions became large billboards on busy (preferably slow-moving) transport routes and more intimate poster panels in retail zones that could intercept people in the act of shopping. Street furniture was designed to adapt poster display to new consumerscapes in shopping precincts and pedestrianized high streets. A good example is the Trilateral illuminated poster display unit, which won a Council of Industrial Design award in 1968: a boxy structure of steel and concrete that mirrored the architectural rhythms of redeveloped town centres (plate 24). In 1969 two billboard companies (More O'Ferrall and London and Provincial) joined forces to form Adshel, to bring a new model of bus-shelter advertising to the UK (pioneered by JCDecaux in France). The idea was that the company carried the cost of designing, installing and maintaining bus shelters on behalf of local authorities in return for the rights to

advertise on them with six-sheet poster panels. It was a crucial shift for billboard companies in morphing from offenders against public amenity to providers of civic infrastructure. Bus-shelter advertising in the UK became especially relevant in the late 1980s, when policies of privatization and contracting out public services had high currency, and local government budgets were being slashed.

During the 1950s and '60s the poster had undergone seismic changes. New approaches and technologies had changed how posters were assembled and a new cast of design and advertising professionals had taken centre stage. Within the advertiser's arsenal, posters had become, as Abram Games put it, 'a strategic reserve rather than heavy artillery, to be used as sparingly as possible'.[24] Within the environment they had been brought under control, beaten back and tidied up. While this adds up to a partial narrative of decline, the following section looks at the areas of advertising and graphic design where the poster continued to enjoy a prominent profile in Britain.

THE CONTINUING POWER OF THE POSTER

In 1969 the now famous 'Pregnant Man' poster promoting birth control was enjoying its moment of public controversy (plate 25). It was one of the first posters issued by the new Health Education Council (HEC), a body set up with the express purpose of importing the techniques of modern advertising into public health strategy: an indication that the emphasis of public health was shifting from social and environmental factors to a focus on the behaviour of the individual. Contributing factors in this were the acknowledgement in the mid-1960s of the health risks involved in smoking and changes in British laws governing sexual behaviour. As society became more legally permissive, the surveillance of sex moved on to the medical agenda.[25] During the early and mid-1960s, public interest advertising had remained one of the bastions of a traditional style of 'soft-sell' poster design. Many COI commissions were carried out by Reginald Mount and Eileen Evans (the Mount/Evans partnership), tried and tested freelance designers who had established their reputations during the war. The HEC, however, turned to a young advertising consultancy, Cramer Saatchi, for a deliberately more aggressive approach to health publicity. As Virginia Berridge writes, 'citizens who would act responsibly if given "the facts" were replaced by consumers of harmful goods or substances who needed to be persuaded about risk'.[26] Subsequent high-profile campaigns addressed smoking, drink-driving, wearing a seatbelt (before it became law) and, more recently, alcohol consumption.

The 'Pregnant Man' poster was shocking because it dealt publicly with the traditionally taboo subject of birth control and did it with the irreverent brio of commercial advertising. The image of male pregnancy was iconoclastic (although it underscored the assumption that the woman's natural position was pitiable and powerless). In its early days, the HEC budget only ran to brochures and poster displays in clinics and local authority sites. The news story that 'Pregnant Man' created, however, extended the reach of the campaign with column inches of free editorial coverage. It was an object lesson in the potential for a poster to command public debate and accrue added publicity value.

Plate 25
WOULD YOU BE MORE CAREFUL IF IT WAS YOU THAT GOT PREGNANT?
Cramer Saatchi (art director: Bill Atherton; photographer: Alan Brooking; copywriter: Jeremy Sinclair). Produced for the Health Education Council, 1969
Offset lithograph
V&A: E.1704–2004

Would you be more careful if it was you that got pregnant?

Contraception is one of the facts of life.
Anyone, married or single, can get free advice on contraception from their doctor or family planning clinic.
You can find your local clinic under Family Planning in the telephone directory or Yellow Pages.

The Family Planning Information Service

The cross-over between advertising and public relations became a hallmark of Charles Saatchi's work. Moreover he came to view posters, with their immediate impact and sound-bite quality, as a form of advertising discipline: 'Charles saw everything as a kind of billboard . . . the shortest number of words, the most powerful simple expression of the message'.[27] 'Pregnant Man' boosted Saatchi's reputation and became something of a founding legend for the Saatchi & Saatchi agency he set up with his brother Maurice a few months later and which went on to become one of the giants of British advertising.

It was another poster, this time for the Conservative Party's 1978–9 election campaign, which turned Saatchi & Saatchi into a household name (plate 26). Amongst the full spectrum of press ads and party political broadcasts that Saatchi & Saatchi produced for the Conservatives it was the 'Labour Isn't Working' poster that drew most attention, partly because of the Labour Party's condemnation of it. Claims that the dole queue depicted on the poster was a composite photograph of Saatchi & Saatchi staff were an attempt to muster outrage against the manipulative techniques of advertising being applied in a political context and used to sell a political party 'like a soap powder'. A more prescient complaint was that an emotive image was being used as a substitute for a policy statement: 'the Conservatives' brand might make more impact,' opined the Under Secretary for Employment, John Golding, 'if they told the people what policies they have hidden up their sleeve to combat unemployment'.[28] Negative 'knocking copy' became a default mode for posters at subsequent British elections, which many feel has served to impoverish the political debate. After the election people were quick to credit the poster for the Conservative win: a highly exaggerated diagnosis, but one which implanted the potent idea that a poster could sway the political process.

Advertising was not new to British politics in 1978, but Saatchi & Saatchi took the Conservative campaign to a new level of professionalism as a disciplined, centrally controlled, marketing machine. The successful collaboration signalled an era of greater reliance by politicians on advertising and media experts. As the party traditionally associated with business interests, there was a degree of affinity between the Conservatives and the advertising industry. Labour were initially more squeamish about full-scale political advertising. However, a highly praised campaign by the Boase Massimi Pollitt agency for the Labour-run Greater London Council in 1984, when the Conservative government threatened it with abolition, was seminal in convincing the Labour leadership that modern advertising could work on the Left (plate 27). At the 1987 election media strategists Philip Gould and Peter Mandelson presided over a slick and professional Labour campaign. An addition to the main campaign was provided by the activities of Red Wedge, a collection of anti-Thatcher popular musicians, comedians and artists led by singer-songwriter Billy Bragg and sanctioned by Labour in an attempt to attract the youth vote: another indication that Labour was addressing its presentation and seeking to open new channels of popular communication (plate 28). By 1996 a rebranded 'New Labour' under Tony Blair was felt to have the edge in marketing and public relations and it was the Conservatives' turn to go on the attack against media spin: their infamous 'demon eyes' poster suggested there were 'dark forces' at work behind the glossy image of Labour's new leader (plate 29). The political posters of the 1990s election campaigns turned into an arms race between the two major parties. Posters were part of the election circus, with poster unveilings staged to provide photo-opportunities, grab headlines and get the message syndicated

THERE IS ONLY ONE LOONY LEFT...

Get rid of her on June the 11th... USE YOUR VOTE ✕

Printed and published by Red Wedge 39, Chippenham Road LONDON W9 2AH Tel: (01) 289 0445 Design JOHN MORRIS photograph PAUL TREVOR   © 1987.

Plate 28
THERE IS ONLY ONE LOONY LEFT . . . GET RID OF HER ON JUNE THE 11TH . . . USE YOUR VOTE
John Morris using a photograph by Paul Trevor, issued by Red Wedge, 1987
Offset lithograph in black and green
V&A: E.109–1996

This poster counters a campaign in the British tabloid press that characterized the more radical elements of the Labour Party as the 'Loony Left'. It shows Conservative Prime Minister Margaret Thatcher staring in an unhinged manner from a television screen.

through the press. In some cases a poster barely appeared on the street but was encountered almost exclusively through the newspapers. Nevertheless, since party political broadcasts on television are carefully limited in Britain with each party allotted equal air time, posters have remained an important way for politicians to address the electorate directly without the mediation of news reporters and editors (televised leader debates were not introduced until 2010). Elections are geographically fought battles and national poster campaigns can be targeted with blanket coverage in marginal constituencies. Billboards are seen as an arena where one party can out-advertise the other in terms of sheer surface area and where the size of their election war chests can tell. In the 1996–7 campaign the Conservatives and Labour lavished around four-fifths of their advertising budgets on posters.

The appearances of political parties on television were restricted, but some products were banished altogether. Cigarette advertising was banned from television in Britain in 1965 and in 1976 regulations were put in place governing which sorts of magazine it could appear in. Advertisements for alcoholic spirits were also withdrawn from television in 1965, this time through a voluntary agreement with the manufacturers. Posters were therefore a crucial platform for big-budget tobacco and liquor advertising accounts (plates 30 and 31). Further restrictions governed the content of cigarette advertisements, which were not permitted to associate smoking with business or social success or with young people, celebrities or nature. Denied

Plate 29
NEW LABOUR, NEW DANGER
M&C Saatchi. Produced for the
Conservative Party, 1997

This was the first and only party
political poster in Britain to
be vetoed by the Advertising
Standards Authority (ASA).
Political parties have never been
subject to the same regulations
as other advertisers on honesty
and truthful representation.
Instead this poster was
withdrawn on grounds of
privacy for its defamatory
representation of Tony Blair. In
2000 the ASA announced that it
would no longer take any part in
regulating political advertising.

Plate 30 (above)
BIRD CAGE
Collett Dickenson Pearce
(art director: Alan Waldie;
photographer: Brian Duffy)
for Gallaher Ltd. Produced for
Benson & Hedges cigarettes,
1977
Colour offet lithograph, c.1977
V&A: E.359–1982

recourse to their now familiar lifestyle themes, advertisers were forced to make a creative leap and find more oblique ways to present the message. The advertisements that Collett Dickenson and Pearce created for the Benson & Hedges 'Pure Gold' campaign focused on the brand's gold packet as a fetishistic object in a series of surreal situations where nothing is quite what it seems. Compulsory government health warnings made advertising copy incongruous (paradoxically the health warnings helped identify the subject of the advertisement as a cigarette product) and the advertisements were delivered through image alone. Billboards for Benson & Hedges, and later Silk Cut (which did not even show the packet), became a mark of the sophistication that British advertising had attained and the level of visual literacy that could be expected from the public in reading images. Edward Lucie-Smith reproduced a Benson & Hedges advertisement in his book *Art in the Seventies* (1980), observing that these billboards were 'more allusive, more decorative and capable of evoking a wider range of associations and responses' than most intentional works of public art.[29] In 2003, when a ban came into effect on all cigarette advertising and promotion in Britain, it was reported not only in terms of health and politics, but as the passing of an era of memorable poster campaigns (plate 32).

Some of the most iconic advertising posters of the 1970s, '80s and '90s in Britain were produced when agencies were pushed to think beyond television. Other stand-out billboard campaigns conceived of their task in terms of creating an episode in public. A notable example is the 1994 Playtex advertisement featuring model Eva

Plate 32 (right)
A Silk Cut advertising event staged in front of billboard posters by M&C Saatchi. On the eve of the ban on cigarette advertising (14 Februrary 2003), Silk Cut reprised the theme of its famous poster campaign featuring slashed purple silk. An image of a large female opera singer dressed in the iconic fabric illustrated the popular saying, 'It's not over till the fat lady sings', and gave cigarette advertising in Britain its swansong.

Plate 33
**HELLO BOYS. THE ONE AND
ONLY WONDERBRA**
TBWA (art director and
copywriter: Nigel Rose;
photographer: Ellen von
Unwerth). Produced for
Playtex UK Ltd, 1994
Offset lithograph,
V&A: E.872–1997

Herzigova greeting her Wonderbra-enhanced cleavage ('Hello Boys') (plate 33). This hit a nerve of post-feminism in popular culture – soon to be followed by the pop band the Spice Girls. While the sexual objectification of women in advertising had been a subject of feminist criticism in the 1970s and '80s (with lingerie billboards a target of graffiti), Wonderbra's provocatively exhibitionist billboard campaign positioned itself as a knowing, ironic take on the mode of the sexist ad and women were expected to get the joke. The campaign suggested, controversially, that it was now permissible and even empowering for women to present themselves to gratify the male gaze. The image worked, therefore, not by being shut inside women's magazines (the hosts of most lingerie advertising), but by being writ large in heterosocial public space to be viewed by both women and men. The poster acted as a form of practical demonstration: the female viewer was asked to observe or imagine men's response to the poster in order to appreciate the impact that she could have if she bought and wore a Wonderbra. Urban myths of men crashing their cars while distracted by the poster drove home the point. Wonderbra billboards simultaneously flaunted the impact of a push-up bra and the impact of a high-profile poster campaign. Eva Herzigova became a poster girl for both Playtex and the poster industry.

For the global brands that came to the fore in the 1990s outdoor advertising was a way to announce their arrival, to lay claim to territory and to make the brand feel locally relevant through physical proximity to people's lives. Multinational brands served by internationally positioned advertising agencies still translate global identities through national references. Nike posters in the UK have successfully traded on the tribal loyalties and edgy nationalism evoked by football in England, and swapped the positivism of their American ads for a dry British wit (plate 34). Nike capitalized on their poster of Eric Cantona and the England flag by producing it as a giant banner, smuggling it into an important match between Manchester United (Cantona's team) and Barcelona and unfurling it in the stadium in front of an estimated television audience of 80 million. Playtex pulled a similar guerrilla-style PR stunt, projecting the Wonderbra advertisement onto Battersea Power Station.

By the late 1990s the advertising picture was beginning to fragment with the multiplication of cable television channels followed by the advent of the internet (see Chapter 3). While this created a myriad of opportunities for niche marketing, media planners began turning back to the poster as a lead 'broadcast' medium to reach a general audience. The adoption of sophisticated systems of audience measurement has made the impact of outdoor advertising appear more quantifiable and attractive to clients. In 1996 the industry set up a specialist body POSTAR (Poster Audience Research) to provide site-by-site estimates of the number of people likely to have 'eyes on' any particular poster. Their methods draw on traffic counts, visibility studies, and scientific research into eye behaviour. Consequently outdoor advertising was no longer regarded as 'a disreputable fag-end of a medium'[30] dominated by drinks and cigarette manufacturers and the government.

Plate 34
'66 WAS A GREAT YEAR FOR ENGLISH FOOTBALL. ERIC WAS BORN
Simons Palmer Denton Clemmow & Johnson (art director: Andy McKay; creative directors: Paul Hodgkinson and Andy McKay; photographers: Norbert Schaner and Seamus Ryan; copywriter: Giles Montgomery). Produced for Nike (UK), 1995
Offset lithograph in black and red
V&A: E.886–1997

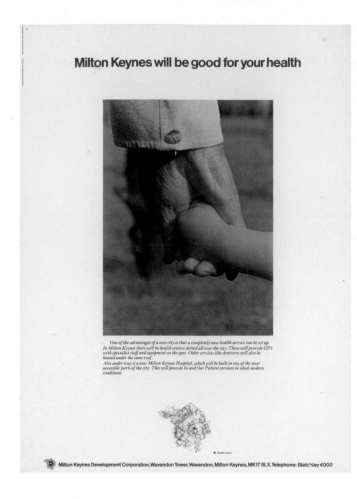

Milton Keynes will be good for your health

One of the advantages of a new city is that a completely new health service can be set up. In Milton Keynes there will be health centres dotted all over the city. These will provide GP's with specialist staff and equipment on the spot. Other services like dentistry will also be housed under the same roof.
Also under way is a new Milton Keynes Hospital, which will be built in one of the most accessible parts of the city. This will provide In and Out Patient services in ideal modern conditions.

Milton Keynes Development Corporation, Wavendon Tower, Wavendon, Milton Keynes, MK17 8LX. Telephone: Bletchley 4000

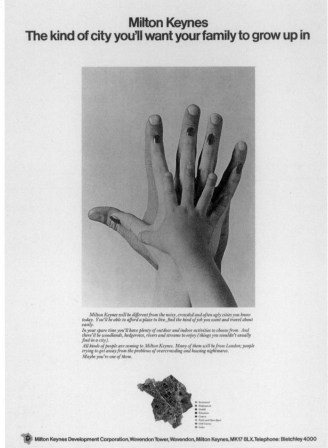

**Milton Keynes
The kind of city you'll want your family to grow up in**

Milton Keynes will be different from the noisy, crowded and often ugly cities you know today. You'll be able to afford a place to live, find the kind of job you want and travel about easily.
In your spare time you'll have plenty of outdoor and indoor activities to choose from. And there'll be woodlands, hedgerows, rivers and streams to enjoy (things you wouldn't usually find in a city).
All kinds of people are coming to Milton Keynes. Many of them will be from London; people trying to get away from the problems of overcrowding and housing nightmares.
Maybe you're one of them.

Milton Keynes Development Corporation, Wavendon Tower, Wavendon, Milton Keynes, MK17 8LX. Telephone: Bletchley 4000

Plates 35 and 36
MILTON KEYNES WILL BE GOOD FOR YOUR HEALTH and **MILTON KEYNES. THE KIND OF CITY YOU'LL WANT YOUR FAMILY TO GROW UP IN**
Minale, Tattersfield, from a series of posters for the Milton Keynes Development Corporation, 1973
Colour offset lithograph
V&A: E.173–2011; E.174–2011

Unable to depict Milton Keynes directly (it was not yet built), Minale, Tattersfield created a series of images for each sector of the city (education, health, business etc) based on human elements (hands in particular) that suggested themes of life and growth.

The poster is a point where the work of advertising agencies and graphic design companies overlap. Nevertheless, the type of poster commissions that each undertake are generally governed by very different sets of priorities. Alex Maranzano of design group Minale, Tattersfield describes it as a question of 'different eyes, different viewpoint, different culture'. Advertising agencies generally handle posters in the context of big-budget advertising campaigns, while a graphic design company or freelance designer is more likely to execute a poster as an extension of an information project: a slower burn, 'quieter' form of poster communication. Examples of the latter are the publicity posters promoting the new city of Milton Keynes as it was being built in the 1970s (plates 35 and 36). These belonged to a large-scale public-information project involving exhibitions, plans and explanatory brochures rather than a quick-sell advertising campaign. The building of Milton Keynes involved human disruption: it absorbed several existing villages while publicity encouraged people in London to uproot and begin new lives in a new city. Architect Derek Walker therefore considered it crucial to maintain a good flow of public information and appointed Minale, Tattersfield, one of the day's most exciting UK design firms, as the project's graphic designers.

The success of the advertising industry in Britain and its advance into more and more areas of life left decreasing pockets of opportunity for posters created within a graphic design milieu. Cultural posters for arts and heritage organizations remained a genre of poster belonging especially to graphic design. Often this has been

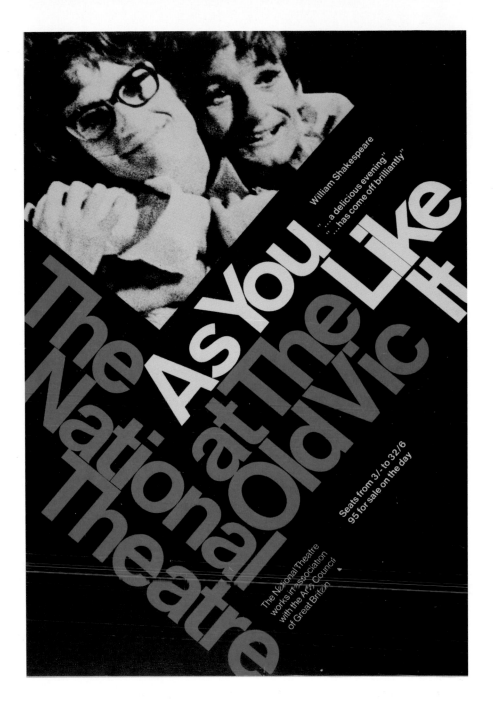

determined both by an institution's limited marketing budgets and a native commitment to good design as part of its cultural offer. Ken Briggs served as a consultant graphic designer for the National Theatre for ten years from its opening in 1963, creating a coherent graphic identity for the new theatre through programmes, booking forms, tickets and a body of posters: often 'Swiss style' compositions of coarse grain photographs and Helvetica Letraset (plate 37). George Mayhew occupied a similar position for the Royal Shakespeare Company. A number of the smaller British galleries, including the Museum of Modern Art (MoMA) Oxford (now Modern Art Oxford), Whitechapel and the Photographers Gallery commissioned adventurous graphic design including posters. Under director David Elliott, MoMA Oxford matched designers to exhibition projects and worked with an impressive portfolio of key figures

LISSITZKY

El Lissitzky **1890 · 1941**

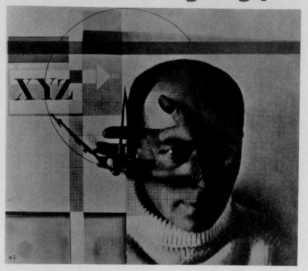

Self-portrait: 'The Constructor'. 1924

From 'Of Two Squares' . 1920

12 June – 10 July 1977 ■
Museum of Modern Art
30 Pembroke Street
Oxford

Tuesday–Saturday 10–5
Sunday 2–5
◆Monday closed

in British graphic design, including Richard Hollis, David King, Malcolm Garrett, Peter Saville and Neville Brody. Elliott saw the poster as an extension of an exhibition project in communicating art and ideas to the public. These galleries produced posters despite limited options for affordable display.[31] Often posters were folded and mailed out along with leaflets and private view cards. Sometimes the poster doubled as a newssheet. An interesting mail-out package could help to generate a buzz and there was always the possibility that the recipient might display the poster on a noticeboard, office wall and so on, thereby spreading the message further (plate 38). Cultural institutions have also turned to posters when they are trying to reposition themselves with the public, often in an attempt to shed an elitist image, such as David Gentleman's series of posters for the National Trust in the mid-1970s (plate 40). The growth of marketing

National Trust

CLIPPED YEW HEDGES, SISSINGHURST CASTLE, KENT

departments and private sponsorship in cultural institutions, however, has tended to make designing a successful poster harder as there are now more parties, often with opposing views, involved in worrying about the design and signing it off. In the 1990s and the early twenty-first century the Johnson Banks design agency was a notable protagonist of the poster in Britain, persuading a range of clients to use posters to communicate in train stations, classrooms and corridors (plate 39). Graphic designers like designing posters and go out of their way to produce them. British design group 8vo sometimes subsidized their own clients by paying for the printing of a poster. 'I don't think anyone really makes money out of designing posters', said Hamish Muir of 8vo in 2002. 'They were a kind of therapy for 8vo – a playground, a chance to be more painterly – to enjoy the magic of working at a large scale'.[32] In other cases designers have used posters to promote their own activities, such as exhibitions, lectures or, in the case of Neville Brody and Jonathan Barnbrook, to showcase a new font. By the 1990s, designers were increasingly challenging the assumption that graphic design is necessarily an exchange between a designer and client, leading to a rise in self-initiated projects and posters created as ends in themselves.

Plate 42 (above)
THIS IS TOMORROW
Theo Crosby for the *This Is Tomorrow* exhibition at the Whitechapel Art Gallery, 1956
Screenprint in black and red
V&A: E.183–1994

Plate 43 (right)
THIS IS TOMORROW
Richard Hamilton for the *This Is Tomorrow* exhibition at the Whitechapel Art Gallery, 1956
Screenprint
V&A: E.176–1994

Plate 44 (below right)
THIS IS TOMORROW
Nigel Henderson for the *This Is Tomorrow* exhibition at the Whitechapel Art Gallery, 1956
Screenprint
V&A: E.179–1994

Chapter 2 | Alternative Directions

POP, PSYCHEDELIA AND THE POSTER BOOM

One of the most iconic images of British Pop Art is a poster. Richard Hamilton created his famous collage 'Just what is it that makes today's homes so different, so appealing?' as a catalogue illustration and exhibition poster for the groundbreaking *This Is Tomorrow* exhibition at the Whitechapel Gallery in 1956 (plate 43). When artists create their own exhibition posters the line between advertising an event and making an artistic statement blurs. This was especially true for *This Is Tomorrow*, where each of the twelve participating groups produced a poster outlining their own particular visual agenda (plates 42 to 44). Hamilton's collage of images from American magazines was a coda to an installation that included billboard-size film posters, a portrait of Marilyn Monroe, a giant Guinness bottle and a 'Robbie the Robot' model from the film *Forbidden Planet*. In retrospect the project seemed to foreshadow the Pop Art ethos, which was to place popular culture on a continuum with high art by embracing the products and printed paraphernalia of mass consumerism as valid subjects of aesthetic interest. And although it was never meant to be an exhibit in its own right, Hamilton's poster/catalogue image was absorbed easily into the canon of British Pop Art.

In 1964 British Pop artists began to make prints which were intended as artworks: in many ways an obvious step for artists fascinated by the qualities of the reproduced image. The catalyst was the Kelpra Press, where a number of Pop artists encountered the process of screenprinting first hand in the course of commissioning exhibition posters. Screenprinting is a technique in which ink is forced through a fabric screen bearing a stencil of the design to be printed. For aesthetic and economic reasons it was to become a crucial process for alternative image-making in the 1960s – both for artists who wanted to work in new ways and (slightly later) for protestors who required a cheap, bold vehicle for their message. Before it was adopted by Pop artists in Britain and America, screenprinting was associated with small print runs of commercial graphic work, particularly posters, and had no fine art pedigree to speak of. This resonance was ideal for Pop Art purposes, as was the smooth, impersonal surface that characterized the medium. While traditional fine art printing techniques such as etching and lithography preserved an autographic sense of the artist's hand, Pop artists were attracted by the mechanical, product-like feel of a screenprint. The results they obtained at the Kelpra Press, working in close collaboration with technician Chris Prater, drew the fine art print and the poster closer together in form. Paolozzi's celebrated 'As Is When' portfolio, published in 1965, included a poster alongside the series of prints screenprinted by the same method on the same stock of paper (plate 45). In 1930s Britain commercial poster printers had shared technology with contemporary artists working in lithography. In the 1960s a fresh, and initially controversial, connection was made through screenprinting.

      The new genre of screenprint art, supported by fine art print publishers such as Editions Alecto and Marlborough, reinvigorated a sagging print market in Britain. A growing public appetite for graphic images to display in the home, however,

Plate 45
AS IS WHEN
Eduardo Paolozzi promoting a portfolio of the artist's prints, published by Editions Alecto, 1965
Colour screenprint
V&A: E.2225–1966

Paolozzi's 'As Is When' series was inspired by the life and writings of the philosopher Ludwig Wittgenstein. It has been hailed as the first masterpiece of screenprinting as fine art.

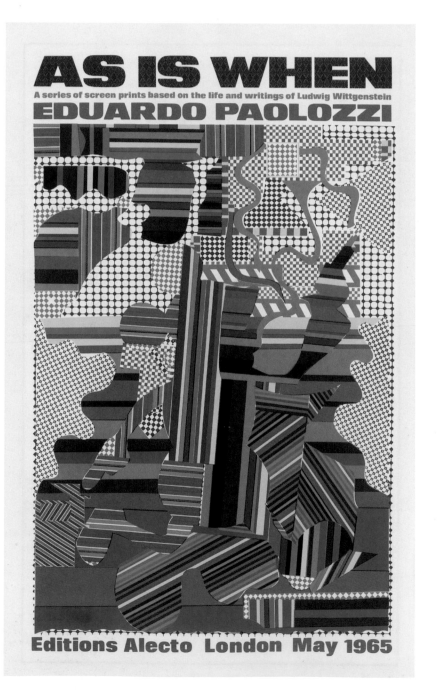

outstripped the market for limited edition prints, which were still relatively expensive. The idea of the poster as the ultimate multiple artwork, or simply as an affordable and edgy decorative statement, fuelled new publishing and retail ventures located in the commercial youth culture emerging in London's Carnaby Street and the King's Road. The first flutterings of a consumer love affair with the poster were evident around 1965 in Tom Salter's trendy Carnaby Street boutique Gear, which was selling comically quaint Victorian advertisements for medicines and corsets blown up to poster size. The poster was revealing its capacity to turn the images picked up by pop culture into a cheap and simple form of merchandise. Graphic works by Alphonse Mucha and Aubrey Beardsley were next in line for poster treatment, following two popular exhibitions at the Victoria and Albert Museum in 1963 (Mucha) and 1966 (Beardsley), which precipitated a surge of interest in Art Nouveau and the art of the 1890s – including its posters.

The same exhibitions had a formative influence on the emerging hippy counter-culture in Britain as it developed a visual style and its own genre of poster art. From 1966 to 1968 a distinctive school of colour-saturated 'psychedelic' posters flowered in Britain, the work of a small handful of designers from within the underground scene. They were commissioned to promote music events and club nights, but moved beyond straightforward advertising to evangelizing the psychedelic experience. Building on the discoveries of Pop (and continuing its voracious process of cultural appropriation), they communicated the peacefully anti-establishment and mind-expanding spirit of the new underground culture, evoking utopian alternatives to the way 'the greys'

(society at large) lived and thought. Designs were a pleasurable decorative riot of erotic figures, fluid letterforms and bastardized Op Art with references to Arthurian legend, Eastern mysticism, Native Americans, fairies, science fiction and drug culture – or, as Michael English (of design duo Hapshash and the Coloured Coat) put it, 'everything that contradicted the rational world' (plates 46 and 47).[1] While their American counterparts were generally printed in large numbers by the offset litho process, screenprint was the economic choice for smaller print runs of British psychedelic posters. The viscose screenprint inks also had the effect of adding colour impact and vibrancy to the designs. The detailed line drawings of London-based psychedelic designer Martin Sharp were reproduced by offset litho, but in this case its flat effect was cheated by printing on foil-coated paper (plate 48). For design observers the illustrative flair of psychedelic posters promised a renaissance in graphic poster art after the encroachment of photography onto commercial billboards. Bevis Hillier concluded in 1969 that 'pure-graphics posters have been given a new and half crazy life, as well as a new status in art . . .'.[2]

Psychedelic posters were initially produced for fly-posting and Nigel Waymouth (the other partner in Hapshash) was exhilarated by the idea of injecting colour into the street, where one of his posters might be seen displayed in repeating blocks outside a club: a blast of ephemeral public art. The entrepreneurs of the underground scene, however, were quick to spot their potential as merchandise and set up production and distribution companies, Osiris Visions and Big O, to supply the posters for personal consumption. People who were never likely to participate actively in psychedelic events were happy to purchase posters inspired by the counter-culture and buy into the style of its beautiful people. A feature by George Melly in the *Observer* in 1967 presented psychedelic posters to an audience outside London's fashionable subculture.[3] The accompanying photoshoot staged what appeared to be an exterior

brick wall plastered in posters, but the hothouse visual effect, the broad selection of pristine poster sheets and an ambience of availability (a caption listed suppliers and stockists) were more suggestive of an interior shop display (plate 49).

The interest surrounding psychedelic posters boosted the already emerging poster market. By 1967–8 posters were staple ware in hip boutiques and alternative bookshops, and an infrastructure of publishers, pundits and retailers dedicated to selling them had developed: a phenomenon that became known as the 'poster boom'. Former American newspaper editor Bob Borzello ran an import and export business in posters. He selected British posters for the American market: posters for theatre companies, London Transport and the General Post Office proved popular (plate 50), and he claimed he could charge more for anything with London on it.[4] His shop Hang-Up in Islington, meanwhile, stocked hundreds of poster titles from around the world, including Polish circus posters and German cinema posters. He even tried to negotiate a supply of Soviet propaganda posters. New publishers like Splash and For Posters produced catalogues of 'pseudo posters' by sourcing images to turn into posters or by commissioning graphic art from scratch. Their products were destined for the decoration of domestic interiors, the walls of restaurants and hotel lobbies.

The obvious influence of Art Nouveau artist Mucha on the psychedelic poster designers encouraged comparisons with the poster craze of the 1890s when, as the V&A's 1963 Mucha catalogue reminded people, the status of the poster 'rose to such a point that the best examples were regarded as works of art on the level of portfolio prints . . . '.[5] As in the 1890s, the flurry of interest in posters encouraged connoisseurship, which was exercised through collecting and new scholarship on the poster during the late 1960s and early '70s.[6] This time round, however, the mania for posters commanded a far wider popular and commercial field, filling a middle ground between original artists' prints and the post-war trend for reproductions of paintings with mass-market appeal (exemplified by Vladimir Tretchikoff's 'Green Lady'). Interviewed in 1968, Philip Townsend (founder of poster publisher Splash) attributed the poster boom to the simple fact that 'people are becoming more graphically aware'.[7] The rich flow of advertisements, colour supplements and television in the 1960s had created a public who were receptive to graphic images and ready to apply them to their own walls.

Plate 51
BABE RAINBOW
Peter Blake multiple
for Dodo Designs, 1968
Colour screenprint on tin
V&A: E.35–2006

Since 'Babe Rainbow' was printed on tin, many people displayed it in bathrooms and kitchens: where paper posters were easily spoiled. It was printed in a run of 10,000 and sold for £1 by Dodo Designs, a company specializing in quirky ornamental homeware.

KISS KISS

Go to work on an egg
bounce a cheque on an egg
wipe your arse on an egg
fail your test on an egg
despair on an egg
overthrow the government
on an egg
dance on an egg
bury your mother on an egg
get sacked on an egg
have a jarthur on an egg
kick an immigrant on an egg
vote Tory on an egg
get high on an egg
go to gaol on an egg
fall in love on an egg
come home and find
a black man in bed
with your wife on an egg
grow bald on an egg
go mad on an egg
love Jesus on an egg
drop napalm on an egg
go to the moon on an egg
write a poem on an egg
have your car repossessed
on an egg
get an ulcer on an egg
get laid on an egg
drop dead on an egg
get stuffed on an egg
go to hell on an egg
kiss kiss.

Christopher Logue with Tom Salter.

A GEAR POSTER © CHRISTOPHER LOGUE PUBLISHED BY FULHAM GALLERY LONDON

Artists looking for new ways to work responded to the poster boom, taking up posters as a form of anti-art or as a means of distributing their work to a wider public through the mass market. Interviewed in 1968, poet Christopher Logue described 'a fantastic upsurge of people doing posters just as creative objects which just are by their very nature multiples' (a term coined in the 1960s for artworks intended to be produced in a large number of copies).[8] He himself pioneered a trend for poster-poems, which used the poster format (a natural composite of words and images) as a piece of multi-media art on which a poet and an artist collaborated (plate 52). It was a way of publishing poetry that tapped into the vogue for graphic art ('an obvious extension of graphic activity').[9] Logue found that the ephemeral, irreverent form of a poster suited his iconoclastic approach and verbal, slangy style, allowing him 'to go public' and challenge the preciousness of his artform:

> I simply feel that I'd like to publish all my poems as posters. For one thing
> it is easier for people who don't associate themselves with book poems,
> which is the majority of us . . . The person with a poem on the wall can
> make the bridge between the words by the person called A. Poet and
> Paul McCartney who is not meant to be that kind of thing.[10]

Poster poems were often printed in both limited and trade editions and, more than any other kind of poster, they bridged the gap between Carnaby Street and the arts. They were sold in large numbers by Gear of Carnaby Street and exhibited in more rarefied form by the Fulham Gallery at the 1968 Brighton Festival.[11] In 1968 Editions Alecto set up its own imprint, Ad Infinitum, for poster-poems, matching poets with a number of the artists it represented. In this case the poster poem provided a template for established print artists to dip a toe in the poster medium and its popular current.

An article in the *Daily Telegraph Magazine* in 1968 noted that 'Posters are selling in a very pop way', concluding that the poster is 'expendable art, the perfect child of the consumer age, that costs as little as five shillings to five pounds, can be thrown away when you are tired of it, framed if you want it forever'.[12] Pinning up posters (Blu-Tack appeared in the 1970s) offered a quick, cheap and peculiarly temporary way to transform a domestic interior. In these terms the poster mirrored a new approach to clothes in the 1960s, when fast-changing and flippant youth fashions were challenging traditional standards of adult taste and durability. The parallel was made explicit in the form of Harry Gordon's disposable poster dresses (plate 53). When you are bored with wearing your poster dress the packet suggested: 'why not . . . cut open all the seams and hang it on your wall as a poster . . . or cover pillows . . . or as your collection grows, sew them together to make a bedspread or curtains or a table cloth'. In furniture, the same impulse towards novelty and easily reconfigured domestic space was evident in the introduction of flat-pack designs, inflatable chairs and beanbags.

For the young in particular, posters expanded the options for decorating personal environments. They gave teenagers an autonomous means of changing their bedroom walls and inscribing their own space inside the family home (paint or wall paper normally required parental consent and funds). Indeed the casual way in which a poster could be replaced was entirely appropriate to the evolving nature of adolescent identity and the need to experiment with different possible selves. For students (a growing demographic as access to higher education expanded in the 1960s), buying

POSTER · DRESS

TRADE MARK

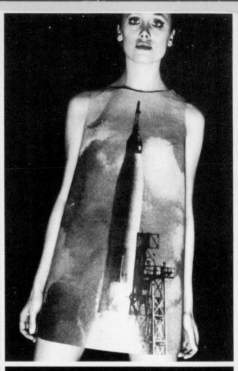

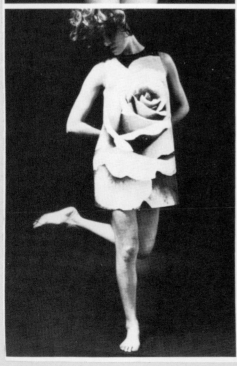

POSTER ® DRESSES
1ST EDITION

Photographs: Marc Leonard

Allen Ginsberg poem courtesy of Cape Goliard Press, London

and hanging posters became part of the ritual of moving into a rented bedsit or a room in a hall of residence: making an alien environment home and inventing themselves in a new phase of life. At a more upmarket level, posters were an option for design-conscious young householders and the expansive scale of a poster suited the proportions of the knocked-through, open-plan living spaces that were becoming fashionable. Gallery Five promoted its range of poster 'wall panels' by photographing them as the centrepieces of different interior design moods supported by matching accessories (a sinuous vase of lilies for one of Aubrey Beardsley's *Salome* illustrations, a vintage trunk and blanket for Ford Madox Brown's *The Last of England* and so on) (plate 54).

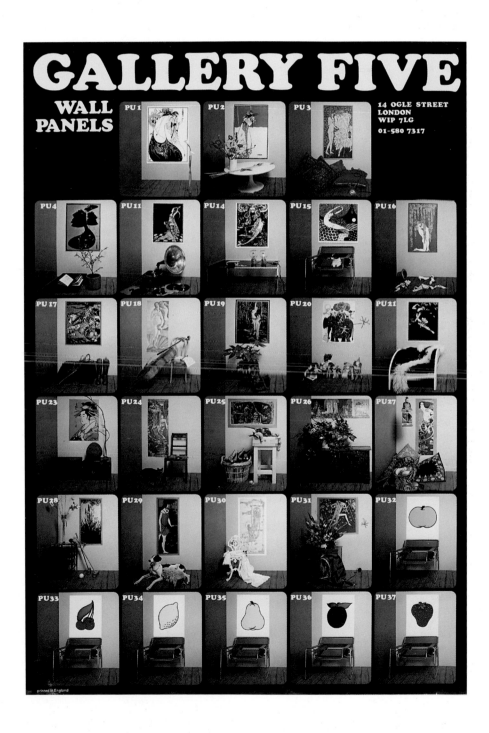

Aside from their decorative qualities, posters allowed you to make events, places, personalities and so on present in your home. Writing in 1970 about the domestication of the poster, Susan Sontag described how posters 'furnish a portable image of the world. A poster is like a miniature of an event: a quotation – from life, or high art.' A personal selection of posters becomes a form of vicarious cultural tourism: 'a set of souvenirs of imaginary experiences'.[13] The posters on your walls were a way of sampling cultural reference points, pulling them into your own orbit and displaying your savoir faire to others.

The name that came to dominate the poster's trajectory as mainstream wall art in Britain was Athena: a shop that opened in Hampstead in 1964 and transcended the boutique model to become a British high street chain in the 1970s and '80s, long after the euphoria of Pop and the poster boom had died away. Until it went into receivership in the late 1990s, Athena remained carefully aligned with the teen market: 'Think of Athena Posters,' recalled one journalist. 'You think of being a teenager, a student, covering walls with Blu-Tack and fantasies and defiance . . . '.[14] Their most popular lines included enigmatic red-lipped women, dreamscape dolphins (or unicorns) and moons, Tutankhamun, cats, chimps on toilets, cars, film spin-offs and pop stars. In the 1980s, Athena defined a hyper-real style of airbrushing that became part of the look of the decade. There were also black and white photographic posters which mimicked the presentation of artworks, with white borders, titles and photographers' signatures. Two of Athena's most iconic posters, both trading on mild sexual fantasies, remain firmly lodged in our collective psyche: 'Tennis Girl' in 1977 and 'L'Enfant' (or Man and Baby) in 1986 (plate 56). Athena posters are one of the 'hidden' genres of mass-market art: the art that most people choose to encounter every day on their walls. They continue to fascinate us as archetypal best-selling pictures that we feel ought to reveal something of the *zeitgeist* of their time. Between the late 1960s poster boom and the demise of Athena, the poster had mutated into a new kind of creative consumer object.

BOYCOTT THE CIRCUS

—————

IT'S CRUEL

PERFORMING ANIMALS' DEFENCE LEAGUE

11 Buckingham Street, Adelphi, W.C.2   TEMple Bar 4080

Director : EDMUND T. MacMICHAEL

ST CHRISTOPHER PRESS LTD., LETCHWORTH, HERTS. *Telephone* 609.

PROTEST POSTER-MAKING

Protest posters were in use in Britain in the late 1940s, although few survive. The Performing Animals' Defence League, for example, issued posters pointing out cruel practices and exhorting people to boycott the circus (plate 57). The labour movement in Britain had a tradition of banners and posters, but some felt that the visual arts had little relevance to the working-class struggle. During the 1960s and early '70s dedicated political artist and posterman Ken Sprague persuaded the British trade union movement to work with him in promoting its cause. The Mountain and Molehill agency he set up with Ray Bernard in 1959 produced posters for most of the UK trade unions throughout the 1960s and '70s and succeeded in giving hearts and minds publicity a new prominence in union work.[15] The early years of the Campaign for Nuclear Disarmament (CND, founded in 1958), meanwhile, heralded a new kind of political mobilization in Britain that circumvented the established channels of party politics, lobbying and trade unionism. Based instead on mass participation and non-violent direct action, CND's visibility was crucial. It combined the spectacle of public marches with a strong logo (which became a new international symbol for peace) and posters by notable (and sympathetic) graphic designers such as F.H.K. Henrion, Ken Garland and Robin Fior (plate 58).

It was the transformatory experience of the student movement (an international phenomenon in the late 1960s) that truly established the role of the poster in grassroots protest in Britain, galvanizing a generation of art students and activists in pursuit of new forms of politics and culture. When art critic and historian Bevis Hillier pronounced 1968 'the year of the poster', he had one eye on the booming trade in psychedelic posters in Britain and America and the other on a wave of agit-prop posters created during an extraordinary year of student revolt around the world.[16]

Plate 57 (opposite)
**BOYCOTT THE CIRCUS,
IT'S CRUEL**
Unknown designer for the
Performing Animals' Defence
League, c.1948
Letterpress in red

Plate 58
**ALDERMASTON TO LONDON
EASTER 62**
Ken Garland for the Campaign
for Nuclear Disarmament (CND)
Offset lithograph, 1962
V&A: E.2699–2007

Ken Garland produced a
number of posters for CND
between 1962 and 1966. This
poster repeats the CND logo
to create the impression of
marching placards.

Paris art students participating in the riots of May 1968 led the way, occupying the studios of the Ecole des Beaux-Arts, setting up the Atelier Populaire (the People's Press) and supplying a rapid stream of posters in support of anti-government strikes. They drew bold monochrome designs which they printed themselves with minimal resources of screenprint equipment and newsprint paper. This paradigm of spontaneous guerrilla poster-making was repeated throughout the year during the Prague Spring, student protests surrounding the Mexico City Olympic Games and anti-Vietnam War demonstrations across numerous cities and campuses around the world. In the radical milieu of 1968, improvised DIY poster-making became part of the toolkit of 'New Left' activism. Inspiration also flowed from Cuba and China, which both produced posters in the late 1960s and early '70s as components of seemingly vibrant revolutionary cultures. Chinese posters were available in Britain and many left-wing activists responded to their powerful brand of optimism, unaware of the brutal reality of China's Cultural Revolution. The Cuban posters, with their bold fields of colour, meanwhile provided a more visually sumptuous model than the linguistic wit of the French student poster-makers.

In London the example of the Atelier Populaire was immediately evident in posters printed during the occupation of Hornsey College of Art when students and staff staged a six-week sit-in from May to July 1968, demanding more flexibility in art and design education and changes in college administration. The Hornsey Graphics Department remained in the hands of the authorities during the occupation, which meant posters-makers had to use any means available, often linocut (plate 59). This rough means of gouged-out image-making, however, satisfied the energy of the moment. Martin Walker described how 'the dawn often saw strange, stray, silent figures still doing battle, ankle deep in lino chippings' and the evolving display of

ISSUED BY AMHCA

posters in the corridors 'echoed the constantly fluctuating debate, and the spontaneity of the situation'.[17]

A number of British activists had travelled to France to witness the events of May 1968 and returned inspired to create a similar revolutionary situation at home. The Poster Workshop, which screenprinted posters from a basement in Camden Road, London from 1968 to 1970, was conceived as part of this effort (plate 60). It was run by volunteers: young British radicals, former art students, a Tunisian sculptor expelled from France for his part in the Atelier Populaire, an ex-merchant navy man working in the dry cleaner's opposite and 'Scriv', a local pensioner, who proved to be a cornerstone of the operation. A list of the Workshop's users demonstrates the

Plate 61

**WE ONLY FEEL THE CHAINS
WHEN WE START TO MOVE**

Red Dragon Print Collective,
1976
Colour screenprint
V&A: E.915–1976

The work of the Red
Dragon Print Collective was
characterized by vivid blocks
of screenprint colour, recalling
the visual richness of Cuban
posters. This poster supports 14
peace activists put on trial for
conspiracy to cause disaffection
amongst British soldiers
serving in Northern Ireland.

spectrum of a reinvigorated libertarian left in Britain, revealing both a groundswell of
community activism and a developing traffic of international causes. These included
groups with local grievances (tenants' organizations protesting against steep rates
rises, strikers from the Ford plant at Dagenham, the Greater London Council Fire
Brigade), ideological organizations (Young Communists, International Socialists),
Black Power movements, Americans dodging the Vietnam draft, civil rights and
freedom movements from around the world (anti-apartheid, the California Farm
Workers Union) and radical film and theatre companies.[18] The Workshop closed in 1970
as its members became more deeply involved in specific political causes. Among
these were Women's Liberation, which, like Gay Rights, emerged as a mass
movement, swelling the wave of activism in British society.

In the early 1970s a politically radicalized subculture developed in Britain, and
especially in London, that was larger and more diverse than many post-1968
underground scenes abroad. It was a mix of resistance and carnival that merged the
playful aspects of 1960s counter-culture with a grittier social anger and a brief
resurgence of grassroots socialism. The backdrop was economic recession and rising
unemployment, industrial unrest, urban decay and social and political crisis. The
troubles in Northern Ireland and the increasingly visible and violent evidence of the
racist far right on British streets contributed to a mood of conflict, and faraway
struggles in South America, southern Africa and the Middle East were brought closer
through news reports, solidarity campaigns and refugee communities.

In this climate radical left-wing poster collectives and community print shops
sprang up across the country, establishing a sustained basis for radical poster

production.[19] Set-ups varied: poster workshops might concentrate on their own propaganda projects, print materials for politically compatible groups, or provide open-door community resources helping people to make their own posters. What they all provided was direct access to basic affordable printing technology and the possibility for a low-tech and oppositional alternative to the sophisticated machine of the mainstream media. As one Poster Workshop notice had put it, printing your own posters was a chance to produce 'information to undermine all that other information – all that $$$$'.

Screenprinting was the backbone of poster-focused projects, while a parallel sector of left-facing service printers offered cheap offset litho printing, which was suitable for community newspapers, campaign literature and badges. In the wake of Pop Art, screenprinting was routinely taught in art colleges and required relatively simple equipment that could be acquired second-hand or even constructed from scratch. Designs could be created by means of hand-cut stencils or by painting directly onto the screen with a resist (a substance that would harden to perform the function of a stencil). Screens could also be prepared photographically, allowing designers to incorporate photographs and found images from books and newspapers. Several workshops built up their own image libraries for this purpose.

In their early days, poster collectives and radical print shops brought together committed individuals and basic equipment in makeshift spaces: insufficiently ventilated basements, garages, derelict shops, even the corners of people's kitchens. For several years the Poster Collective was based in Tolmers Square near Euston railway station – one of the squatter communities in London that occupied housing stock left derelict by property speculators. Here the squatters practised radical resistance as a way of living and, amid the freedoms and sacrifices that this entailed, poster-making (research, design, printing and distribution) could be a full-time operation.

While their frontline function was printing, radical poster collectives and print shops were also experimental spaces and points of connection in the fluid networks of left-wing activism. They were places where people met, argued and exchanged skills; where political beliefs were enacted in microcosm through democratic working structures and where political thinking bled into questions of culture. Motivations ranged from those who simply wanted to use their creative skills in the service of political struggle to those who theorized that changing society implied changing the concept of art and the role of the artist. A keynote of British art in the 1970s was the emergence of a socialist and feminist consciousness among artists.[20] The broad agenda was to challenge art's separation from society in the post-industrial age, replacing the pursuit of art for art's sake, evaluated through the gallery system and the market, with work that prioritized social meaning and direct communication. Poster-making was one way for artists to transform their work in relation to different social environments and audiences. Members of the Poster Collective were mostly ex-staff and students from London art colleges who described themselves as rejecting the traditional role of the artist as 'someone who is negatively free to do anything in the name of art'.[21]

Equally, some left-wing poster artists were wary of creating a 'crude mirror-image' of capitalist advertising or selling socialism as 'just another promise on offer within the system'.[22] The design problem was how to prioritize hard information over sensation and reveal the complexity of an issue in the succinct form of a poster. The

DOORS OF BELFAST ©

POSTER ISSUED BY, AND SOLD IN AID OF THE NORTHERN IRELAND POVERTY LOBBY. DESIGN: PETER McGUINNESS. PRINTED AT ART & RESEARCH EXCHANGE

Plate 62 (opposite)
DOORS OF BELFAST
Peter McGuinness, printed by
the Art & Research Exchange
and issued by the Northern
Ireland Poverty Lobby, 1985
Screenprint in black and silver
V&A: E.170–2011

This poster was part of a
project designed to give graphic
representation to the plight of
the poor in Northern Ireland. It
subverts a well-known tourist
poster 'Doors of Dublin',
which was a compilation of
picturesque and colourful
eighteenth-century doorways.

Plate 63
**CAPITALISM ATTACKS
EDUCATION BECAUSE
EDUCATION DOES NOT
PRODUCE QUICK PROFIT**
Leonard Breen, Juan Munoz
and David Dahlson, produced
for a student occupation of
the Central School of Art and
Design, 1977
Screenprint in orange
V&A: E.929–1977

The message of this poster
is framed in the language of
Marxism. The subversive use
of comic-strip speech bubbles
was a visual tactic associated
with the Situationists, a group
of radical French social and
cultural theorists who were
an influence on the student
revolutionaries in Paris in 1968.

Plate 64
VICTORY TO PFLOAG
Poster Collective (later known
as the Poster Film Collective),
early 1970s
Screenprint
V&A: E.1713–2004

Plate 65
**DEFEND WORKERS'
RIGHT TO ORGANISE**
Poster Collective (later known
as the Poster Film Collective),
issued by the Grunwick Strike
Committee, 1977
Screenprint in red and black
V&A: E.143–2011

A strike by low-paid Asian
women over conditions at the
Grunwick film processing plant
in north London in 1976–8
became a national focus for
the battle between unions and
employers.

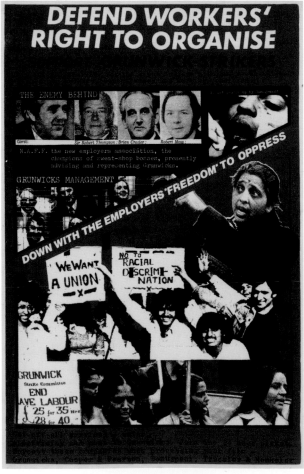

Rajput windows and the ethereal voice of the sitar.
Murals of the legends of Krishna and silks and brocades from Rajasthan.
A glimpse of India on your way to New York.

AIR-INDIA

Ash trays and the extensive dirty floors of the airport.
The arrivals and departure board of Heathrow and the overalls from Acme.
A glimpse of exploitation on your way to New York.

IMMIGRANT-LABOUR

Plate 66
AIR-INDIA. IMMIGRANT-LABOUR
Protest poster reproducing
an artwork by Paul Wombell,
printed by the Poster Collective,
c.1977
Screenprint
V&A: E.928–1978

Poster Collective progressed from single images and bold legends to increasingly layered and didactic compositions of text and image, pushing poster design to the limit (plates 64 and 65). Driven by a desire to say more, some members began working with film and producing sets of posters on historical processes (women's history, colonialism and technology) intended for viewing over a sustained period in environments such as schools. At the same time a new interest in the politics of representation, in decoding and exposing the values and assumptions behind media images, was feeding into the work of socially radical artists.[23] In 'Air-India. Immigrant Labour', Paul Wombell placed an Air India press advertisement featuring a glamorous air hostess beside his own photograph of an Asian cleaner at Heathrow Airport: using documentary reality to puncture an advertising fantasy and render the exploitation of both women visible (plate 66).

Collective authorship was a founding principle of many radical poster projects. It was a stance intended to undermine the accepted idea of an artist as an individual set apart by the 'magical quality' of personal talent and corresponded to Feminism's unfolding critique of art history as a record of the lives and genius of great men. Suzy Mackie, a member of the See Red Women's Workshop recalls how their collective practice ruffled people's understanding of individual agency and competition in the art world: 'You'd bump into somebody you'd met at art school, male usually, who would say, "But I can't understand, who holds the pencil? Who holds the pencil, somebody must hold the pencil?"'[24]

Plate 67
Members of See Red Women's
Workshop, 1980, published in
Spare Rib

Plate 68 (opposite)
DISC JOCKEY
See Red Women's Workshop,
*c.*1974
Screenprint in green
V&A: E.85–2011

See Red's method was design by direct democracy. Artwork and slogans were thrashed out and reworked in group discussion at every stage of the process and no poster left the workshop until all the members were happy with it (plate 67). Individual hands can be discerned in their posters, but no signatures were added. See Red was typical of the small collective units that made up the fabric of the women's movement. Perhaps the most important of these building blocks were the consciousness-raising groups where women came together to voice their feelings and discover commonalities: a powerful strategy in identifying many of the frustrations and miseries in women's private lives as being social and political in origin rather than individual and inevitable. See Red lifted many of the ideas for their posters out of the consciousness-raising groups they attended so that their work was both deeply personal and organically wired into the wider movement. A number of their early designs address women's private domestic lives and are both angry and darkly humorous (plate 68). When they were hung in individual women's homes they preserved the impetus of consciousness raising and served as 'a strong reminder that women share a common struggle, and that we can break out of our isolation'.[25]

Community print shops were a constituent of an expanding community arts movement in Britain and promoted a participatory principle of cultural democracy.[26] This implied widening access to the production rather than the consumption of culture

Plate 69
**FREE CASTRATION
ON DEMAND**
Pen Dalton, *c.*1974
Screenprint in black, blue
and purple
V&A: E.656–2004

Pen Dalton screenprinted
women's liberation posters at
home and sold them through
left-wing book shops and at
conferences. The references in
this design include the savage
wit of Valerie Solanas's SCUM
(Society for Cutting Up Men)
manifesto and Laura Mulvey's
writing on fetishism and
castration fear. Dalton added a
pair of dressmaking scissors as
a domestic reference.

as opposed to either Pop's optimism in the mass market (a Peter Blake multiple) or
Arts Council initiatives to bring elite culture to everyone (Shakespeare in working
men's clubs). As John Phillips of Paddington Printshop explained: 'most of Paddington
culture is to consume, to accept that you can't make a mark on the world; that you're
there and your only pleasure is to say, "I bought"; never to say, "I made".'[27] One strategy
for print shops was to run workshops teaching people the skills needed to print their
own posters – or at least to 'demystify' the technical skills and processes that divided
the specialist from the non-artist (plate 71). Often they worked in close collaboration
with local people to realize their poster needs (from protest campaigns to promoting
local events), and were flexible over how involved people became in the design and
printing, offering a mix of service and self-help. The idea was that a community print
shop could function rather like a letter writer in a pre-literate village: a local port of
call when people needed to put their ideas into graphic form. Paddington Printshop
(still in existence as the London Print Studio) established itself as a centre for
community action in its local area and provided a template for similar set-ups
around the country.

  After the general election of 1979, community print shops stood instinctively
opposed to Margaret Thatcher's ideology of individualism and privatization. In
practical terms they fought the impact her government was having on particular
communities. The Docklands Community Poster Project (DCPP) campaigned over a
period of ten years, opposing the government's redevelopment of Docklands on the

We are a little worried about our landlord.

Plate 70
WE ARE A LITTLE WORRIED ABOUT OUR LANDLORD
John Phillips of Paddington Print Shop for the Walterton and Elgin Action Group, 1986
Colour screenprint
V&A: E.169 2011

Plate 71
PUPPETS ART WORKSHOP
Carol Kenna of Greenwich Mural Workshop, 1976
Screenprint in black, green and purple
V&A: E.100–2011

EVERY TUESDAY
PUPPETS
4~6 P.M.
SILK~SCREEN
6~9 P.M.
ART WORKSHOP
13 COLTMAN HOUSE

Plate 72

A–Z OF A MINER'S WIFE

Dawn Hampson, Janine Head,
Maureen Ward and Artivan for
the Normanton and Altofts
Miners Support Group, 1984–5
Screenprint in black and red on
yellow paper
V&A: E.142–2011

Artivan was a mobile workshop
that worked with communities
around Yorkshire in the 1980s,
including those affected by
the miners' strikes. For many
women in mining communities,
organizing campaigns to
support men on the picket lines
was their first experience of
political action.

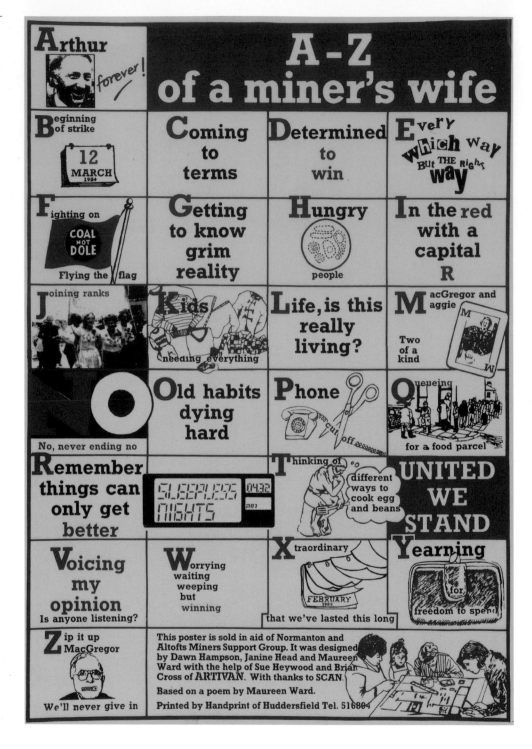

grounds that it favoured the interests of private investors over the needs of the people who lived there.[28] Artists Peter Dunn and Loraine Leeson worked through a steering committee affiliated with a strong network of local tenants' associations and action groups, mapping the poster project onto a remarkable campaigning community in Docklands. Its most spectacular output was a series of photo-mural billboards positioned around the Docklands area: posters 'but large ones to match the scale of the developers' proposals' (plate 73).[29]

THE CHANGING PICTURE OF DOCKLANDS
Community Photo – Mural

THE CHANGING PICTURE OF DOCKLANDS
Community Wall Poster
BIG MONEY IS MOVING IN

THE CHANGING PICTURE OF DOCKLANDS
Community Photo – Mural
BIG MONEY IS MOVING IN

THE CHANGING PICTURE OF DOCKLANDS
COMMUNITY PHOTO–MURAL
SHATTERING THE DEVELOPERS' ILLUSIONS...

Plate 73

**THE CHANGING PICTURE
OF DOCKLANDS**

A series of photo-murals by
the Docklands Community
Poster Project situated around
the Docklands area of Tower
Hamlets. Each was constructed
of portable sections which were
changed a few pieces at a time
so that the image gradually
transformed and provided a
narrative of the issues affecting
the contested redevelopment of
the area.

The struggle to get the billboards up went to the heart of the conflict over
development in Docklands as planning permission had to be obtained from the London
Docklands Development Corporation (LDDC), the body set up to supersede the local
councils and drive ahead the government scheme – effectively disenfranchising
residents at a local level. The LDDC could not legally veto the billboards on grounds of
content and tried to argue, through the rule book, that their appearance would be
detrimental to the amenities of residents – though no resident was consulted. The
DCPP answered with a huge petition proving local support for the community-owned
project and won six cases (out of forty applications) on appeal. The billboards
represented a thorn in the side of the LDDC and a small victory against it. John Phillips
points out that an intrinsic characteristic of radical culture is the illicit occupation of
space: sit-ins, squatting, marching in a demonstration down the middle of a road.[30]
Either in person (carried as placards) or in proxy (pasted on walls), posters were part
of the process of claiming a space and trespassing on the establishment. Even in
Docklands, where the poster project had a hard-won legality, it occupied a format (the
billboard) that was usually the preserve of powerful advertisers and political parties.

Outside the frameworks of community arts and radical collectives, key
individual artists and designers put their weight behind political causes during the
energetic activism of the 1970s and early '80s. Paul Peter Piech's linocut posters were

Plate 74 (opposite)
FALKLANDS – FALKLANDS
Paul Peter Piech, *c*.1982
Linocut in black and blue
V&A: E.773–1986

Piech created this caricature of
British Prime Minister Margaret
Thatcher in protest against the
Falklands War and the way in
which Thatcher derived political
capital from the conflict.

Plate 75
STOP THE NAZI NATIONAL FRONT!
David King, published by the Anti Nazi
League, 1978
Offset lithograph in black and red
V&A: E.197–2011

personal pleas for peace and social justice and his craft-based approach left a palpable impression of an individual hand and conscience (plate 74). The distinctive styles developed by David King and Peter Kennard meanwhile forged strong public profiles for nationwide 'anti' campaigns. After a decade as art editor of the *Sunday Times Magazine*, David King turned his attention to political design in the late 1970s, producing a powerful body of protest posters for organizations including Apartheid in Practice, the Anti Nazi League and Rock Against Racism. He wanted to introduce professional design rigour into what he felt was a mishmash of graphics on the Left. Challenged by tiny printing budgets and tight deadlines, he developed a vocabulary of emphatic type and heavy rules. These elements were masterfully spaced and weighted on the page, but also captured the vernacular energy of letterpress posters advertising boxing bouts. The designs were effective in just two colours and photographic images were made to 'sing' by printing black and red dot-on-dot (plates 75 and 76). The confidence of King's posters matched the Anti-Nazi League's imperative to reach beyond community activism and the committed Left to galvanize a broad base of anti-racist support against the National Front. Printed by offset litho in runs of 70,000 they achieved huge coverage and mounted a counter-offensive against the Front's street displays of racist graffiti, union jacks and bricks through windows (plates 77 and 78).

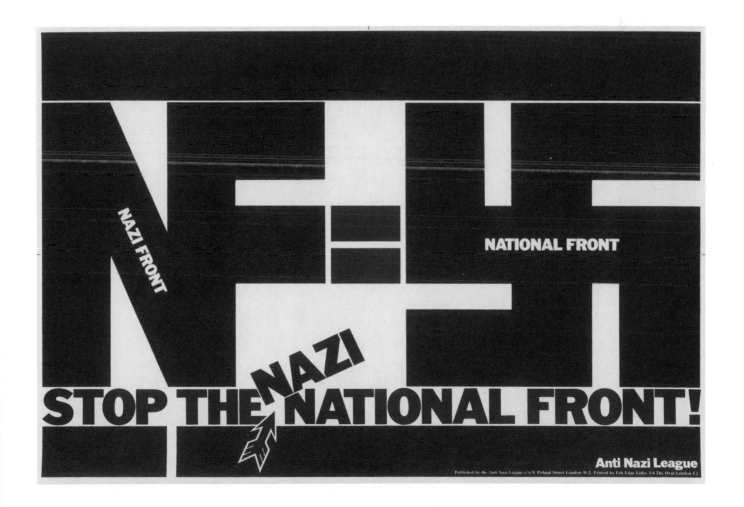

NEVER AGAIN!

Anti Nazi League

Published by the Anti Nazi League c/o 9, Poland Street London W.1
Printed by Feb Edge Litho 3-4 The Oval London E2

STOP THE NF!

Plate 76 (opposite)
NEVER AGAIN!
STOP THE NAZI NF!
David King, published by
the Anti-Nazi League, 1978
Offset lithograph in black
and red
V&A: E.195–2011

Plate 77 (above)
Paul Trevor, photograph
of an anti National Front
demonstration passing through
Curtain Road in the East End of
London, 20 August 1978. One of
the protestors carries a David
King poster on a placard.

Plate 78 (right)
Paul Trevor, photograph of
racist graffiti in Brick Lane in
the East End of London, 1978

NO NUCLEAR WEAPONS

CAMPAIGN FOR NUCLEAR DISARMAMENT
11 GOODWIN STREET LONDON N4·TELEPHONE 01 263 4954

Photomontage by Peter Kennard

Plate 79 (opposite)
NO NUCLEAR WEAPONS
Peter Kennard, for the
Campaign for Nuclear
Disarmament (CND), 1980–1
Offset lithograph in black
and red
V&A: E.328–2011

Peter Kennard writes that the
'point of my work is to use easily
recognizable iconic images, but
to render them unacceptable.
To break down the image of the
all-powerful missile, in order
to represent the power of the
millions of people who are
actually trying to break them.'

Plate 80 (above)
Peter Kennard, photograph of
CND demonstrators carrying his
posters in London, 1981

Peter Kennard's photomontages became the face of a new phase of CND
protest in the early 1980s, following public alarm over NATO rearmament and the
decision in 1979 to station American cruise missiles on British soil (plate 79). Kennard
was an artist who turned from painting to a socialist tradition of photomontage in
response to the student movement of 1968. John A. Walker describes him as one of
the few radical artists of the period whose work could square up to the impact of
contemporary advertising imagery.[31] The images he created for CND were distributed
in newspapers and photo essays and on posters, placards, badges and T-shirts,
earning him the title of 'Britain's unofficial war artist' (plate 80).

In 1988–91, outrage against the government's introduction of the Poll Tax
(a flat-rate tax to finance local government that was not indexed to an ability to pay)
formed into a protest movement on a vast scale, involving millions of ordinary people,
the majority of whom had never been involved in political action before. Anti-Poll Tax
propaganda and demonstrations were more than symbolic declarations designed to
carry public opinion against the government: they incited individuals to resist by
refusing to pay what was widely felt to be an unfair tax. In some areas anti-Poll Tax
posters were plastered over 'every blank space; every lamppost; every street
corner'.[32] Designs were mostly unremarkable, composed of plain text slogans or
baldly militant humour (an image of a savage dog with the tag line 'Bailiffs . . . Make My
Day'), but they played a crucial role in creating the confidence required to break the law
by not paying. The campaign relied on the psychology of safety in numbers (the courts
couldn't jail everyone) and so it needed outward proof of people's invisible breaches of

payment: 'No Poll Tax Here' posters placed in street windows and public burnings of Poll Tax bills reassured non-payers that they were part of a collective action.

The Poll Tax rebellion was an extraordinary instance of mass protest and community action. More generally the seam of activism and radical discourse set in train by the student movement of 1968 had begun to peter out by the mid- to late 1980s. Many campaigning organizations had come to rely on funding from Labour-run local authorities, only to be starved out of existence when local government resources were cut after the 1987 general election. By the early 1990s nearly all the radical and community print shops had closed or changed direction and the activists who ran them had moved on. Bob Geldof's Live Aid concert in 1985 for African famine relief, meanwhile, helped propel popular political action into mainstream media channels. Humanitarian crises, animal rights, environmental concerns and AIDS awareness became subjects for professional billboards and bus-side advertisements. A billboard poster for anti-fur campaign Lynx turned fashion photography against the fur trade and was photographed by David Bailey – one of the stars of the genre (plate 81). It was recognized with a D&AD (Design and Art Direction) award and the concept of professional 'design with a conscience' continued to gain currency throughout the 1990s, to the point where social awareness could become part of brand identity.

At the same time anti-globalization, in tandem with radical environmentalism, emerged as an umbrella movement for a new wave of world-wide activism in which the practices of corporate marketing and global branding were held up to scrutiny. The form of graphic protest most closely associated with anti-globalization is 'subvertising', whereby the advertisements of multinational brands are satirized by being doctored or spoofed. Adbusters, founded in 1989 in Vancouver, became a flagship organization for this kind of creative resistance, propagating subvertising and 'culture jamming' around the world through its magazine, campaigns and competitions. In Britain in the 1990s subvertising took to the streets, with graphic

Plate 81

IT TAKES UP TO 40 DUMB ANIMALS TO MAKE A FUR COAT. BUT ONLY ONE TO WEAR IT

Yellowhammer Advertising Co. Ltd (art director: Jeremy Pemberton; photographer: David Bailey; copywriter: Alan Page), 1986–7
Offset lithograph in black and red
V&A: E.3041–1991

activists Saatchi & Someone and Active Visual Intervention altering billboards with a skilful application of paper and paste, working seamlessly with the visual vocabulary of the host advertisement to turn it against itself (plate 83). In 2000 Adbusters updated and re-issued Ken Garland's 1964 'First Things First' manifesto as a clarion call to designers not to serve blindly the cause of consumerism. The host of professionals who added their signatures demonstrated how the anti-globalization debate had carried a spirit of activism inside the design industry. Subvertising shifted the focus of graphic resistance from creating radical alternatives to mainstream design and advertising to exposing and attempting to reform its practices.

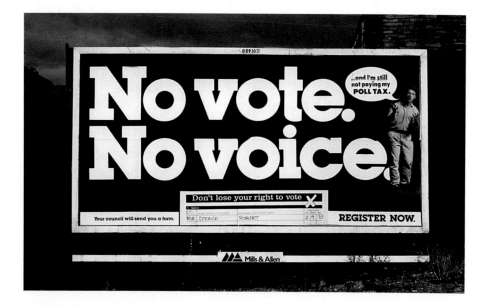

mick english

freakout dec 23/30; under berkeley cinema tot.ct.rd. 10½ pm warhol, pink floyd, anger, heating; it

movies   sounds   movies   warm   god

DEC 23: 10/- +FREE MEMBERSHIP

POSTERS AND POPULAR MUSIC

From the late 1960s onwards, successive waves of music-led youth culture provided a crucible for experimental graphic design in Britain. Writing in 1967, George Melly identified the psychedelic underground, on the evidence of its posters, as 'the first of the pop explosions to have evolved a specifically *graphic* means of expression'.[33] Alongside music and fashion, graphics continued to be one of the building blocks of sub-cultural styles. Psychedelic posters came from designers immersed in the underground scene, looking to translate their own first-hand experience of its music, events and philosophy. Barney Bubbles's close collaboration with the band Hawkwind in the early 1970s further established the idea of the music designer as an involved insider as opposed to the detached problem solver of mainstream graphic design, and independent record labels became the employers or clients of choice for designers who wanted the freedom to work in a more personal and emotional way.

Music posters advertised record releases or live performances (from small underground gigs to grand stadium tours) and were also produced as intentionally

Plate 84 (opposite)
NITE TRIPPER
Michael English, for the
UFO club in London, 1966
Offset lithograph
V&A: E.1695–1991

Dominated by the girl's eyes, this poster focuses on the visual (or visionary) aspect of psychedelic experience. The lettering painted on her face suggests the effect of light projections used by bands like Pink Floyd.

Plate 85
**THE ROLLING STONES
AMERICAN TOUR 1972**
John Pasche, published by
Chipmunk and issued by
Sunday Promotions, 1972
Colour offset lithograph
V&A: E.95–2004

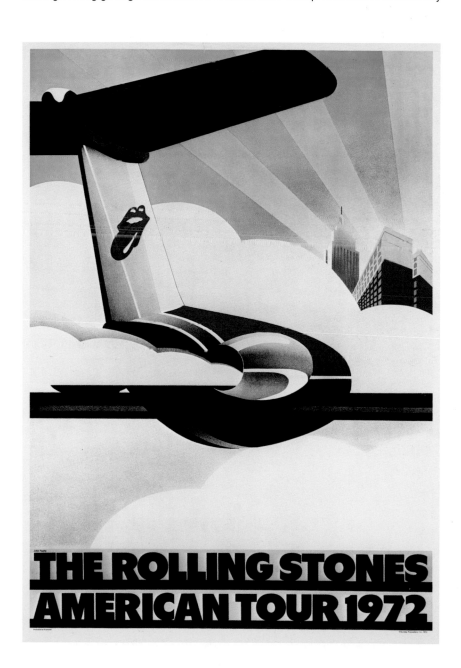

Ian Dury With Love

Plate 86 (opposite)
IAN DURY WITH LOVE
Barney Bubbles,
photography by
Chris Gabrin, 1977
Screenprint in pink,
blue and green
V&A: E.313–2011

One of five posters produced
for a Stiff Records tour, which
were intended to be sold as
merchandise.

Plate 87
THE WHO SELLOUT
Adrian George, published by
Osiris Visions, c.1972
Colour offset lithograph
V&A· F.553–1985

This poster was distributed
inside the LP cover of the
'Sellout' album by the Who.
The largely symmetrical design
plays on the fact that people
would encounter the poster by
untolding it, recalling a form
of children's painting where
one half of a sheet of paper
is daubed with paint and then
folded to imprint a mirror
image.

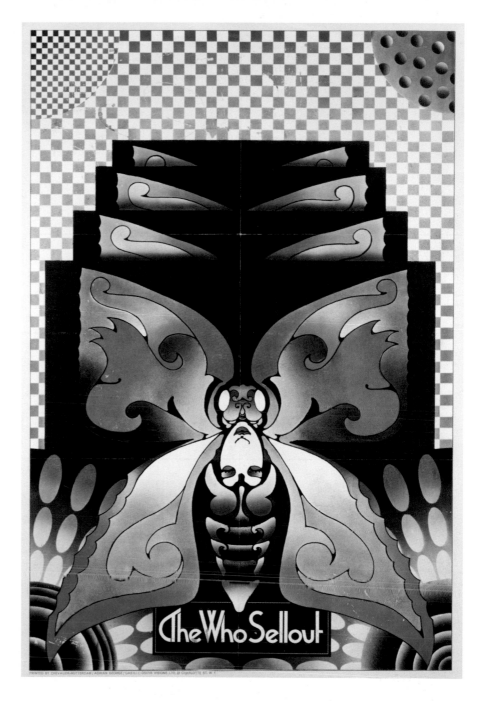

collectable objects, sometimes distributed as an added extra in the album package.
However, it was the LP (long play) sleeve that provided the economic and creative
centre of gravity for much music design. Posters promoting record releases and
related gigs were frequently assembled simply by reframing the sleeve art and finding
something to do with the strip of space created when a square record cover becomes
a rectangular poster (plate 88). Album covers, meanwhile, became increasingly
complex confections involving double gatefold structures, cut-outs, fold-outs, and
inserts. Such embellishments all added to the pleasure of unpacking the record.
This was turned to humorous account in the Rolling Stones' *Sticky Fingers* album
cover (designed by Andy Warhol) which featured a man's crotch in tight blue jeans
with a working zipper revealing underpants on the inner sleeve.

Punk, reacting against this kind of elaborate production, was a moment of creative energy for the poster. Emphasis on the immediacy of performance made walls as important a site for graphics as record sleeves, while street publicity was essential for an outsider style that got limited television and radio play. Posters fitted the raw outdoor aesthetic of punk. Designs spoke of a degraded urban environment referencing graffiti lettering, tattered fly-posters and smashed windows. Flimsy paper (like torn fabric) was an eloquent punk material and was flaunted by devices such as cut-out 'ransom note' lettering and rough collages reproduced bare of sophisticated printing finishes. In an attempt to keep their product affordable, anarchist punk band Crass packaged several of their records wrapped in posters rather than sleeves (plate 90). By rejecting technical virtuosity in musicianship and design, Punk moved to collapse the gap between a band and its fans. This DIY stance had a familial link with community print shops,[34] but while the latter were sometimes divided over the importance of design quality within their mission, punk's statement was purposefully anti-design. The deliberately untutored and easy-to-achieve appearance cultivated by punk designers inspired many genuine amateurs to create their own posters and

Plate 88
I'M NOT PERFECT (BUT I'M PERFECT FOR YOU)
Richard Bernstein, promoting a recording by the rock singer Grace Jones, *c.*1987
Colour offset lithograph
V&A: E.163–1987

The sleeve art for the Grace Jones single 'I'm Not Perfect (But I'm Perfect For You)' is reproduced on this poster. Strips of the original square image have been repeated to fill a poster format – a device that helps convey the advertised extended remix of the song.

fanzines armed with no more than paper, scissors, felt marker and access to a high street print shop or photocopier.

Rock Against Racism (RAR) sought to fuse the subversive energies of radical politics and music in late 1970s' Britain and create an 'emotional alternative' to far right nationalism. RAR staged events in which reggae and punk rock acts shared the billing, bringing together the young black and white fan bases belonging to the two different musical forms.[35] Punk was an ambiguous movement in terms of politics and RAR sought to deny it as a potential cultural stomping ground for National Front skinheads. Graphics and graphic designers were a driving force in RAR's mobilization, and its printed products (badges, stickers, posters and banners) set out the political context in which the bands appeared (plate 91). The name of RAR's newspaper, *Temporary Hoarding* (described as 'half poster, half illustrated lyrics with some politics in between'), evoked the spirit of fly-by-night illegal street posters and was a tribute in particular to the tactics of the pro-democracy movement in China, which was papering Chinese cities in wall posters (*dazibao*) during the 'Beijing Spring' of 1978.

In the post-punk 'new wave' era record labels provided patronage for a number of important British graphic designers who were influential in challenging mainstream conventions: Malcolm Garrett, Peter Saville, Neville Brody and Vaughan Oliver. All are known for famous album covers, but their approach to designing for music often encompassed the presentation of a band as a total project. Garrett described his vision

Plate 90
Gee Vaucher and Penny
Rimbaud, inside of the poster
sleeve for the album *Stations of
the Cross*, Crass Records, 1979
Offset lithograph
V&A: E.1208–1988

involving 'how the band looked on stage . . . how their merchandising was sold, how the records were advertised, how the street posters were done, how the sheet music was sold, everything'.[36] Vaughan Oliver loved the poster as a form (with particular reference to the Polish Poster School and the work of Japanese designer Tadanori Yokoo) and insisted that it should be respected as a separate entity from the LP sleeve, with its own proportions and scale: needing to work from across the street rather than weighed in the hand. He often avoided reproducing the sleeve image on a poster, preferring to rework the visual elements of a project from scratch to create a more interesting slippage between album and poster (plate 94).

If album covers were suited to close-up encounters in music shops and personal record collections, the music poster held sway on the street. Gig posters with black text on fluorescent paper were ubiquitous and preceded a band's arrival in town. Music advertisers were the bread-and-butter clients of the highly organized and lucrative illegal fly-posting business. Printed posters were handed over (usually in a car park) to territorial fly-posting gangs, controlled by underground characters such as Terry 'the Pill' Slater. Martin Hannett describes the process: 'The poster bandits used to rocket around the country at all hours of the day and night, for weeks at a time. They were like Weavers, they used to light their joints with ten pound notes, the poster men.'[37]

The significance of record industry graphics declined as the LP was replaced by the smaller format CD (in the late 1980s) and cover art shrank in size. The CD booklet viewed from behind the brittle plastic of a 'jewel case' cover did not command the visual or tactile appeal of the LP sleeve and poster design also lost out amid a general

Plate 91
**SOUTHALL KIDS ARE
INNOCENT**
Syd Shelton and Ruth Gregory,
for a Rock Against Racism
benefit concert, 1979
Screenprint on pink paper

flux3

the edinburgh new music festival

2nd week

jaffacake 8/97

sun 17 strike out 4 (at 13.00)
tue 19 urusei yatsura/mogwai/
the delgados
wed 20 tindersticks
thurs 21 faust
fri 22 composers ensemble
sat 23 acid brass
sun 24 heaven 17

doors 20.00

tickets fringe 0131 226 5138
inside tickets 0131 477 8222

a usp arts presentation

Plate 92 (opposite)
**FLUX: THE EDINBURGH NEW
MUSIC FESTIVAL**
8vo, 1997
Colour screenprint

Plate 93
THE FACTORY
Peter Saville, for Factory
Records, promoting a night
at the Russel [sic] club,
Manchester 1978
Screenprint in black and yellow

Plate 94
BLOW
Vaughan Oliver, with
photography by Dominic
Davies and Chris Bigg, for 4AD
promoting an album by the
band Swallow.
Colour offset lithograph

FREE FESTIVAL
PRAG (CZECH REP.)
28.7 to 2.8.94

SPIRAL TRIBE
SOUND SYSTEM

MUTOID WAST
COMPANY

INFOLINES

PRAG (czech rep.): (42) 2.725862
(42) 2.879969
PARIS (france): (33) (1) 40111547
(33) (1) 49190112

INVITATION
TO A
UNDERGROUN
SOUND SYSTE
ARTISTS A

Plate 95 (opposite)
FREE FESTIVAL
Melanie Wilson,
Spiral Tribe flyer, 1994
Photocopy

Plate 96 (above)
Photograph by Natalie Bates of
rave flyers stuck floor to ceiling
on her bedroom wall, early
1990s.

Teenagers too young to attend
raves would collect the flyers
as a way of being part of the
scene. They were picked up
from small record shops and
different designs were swapped
at school.

reduction of creative interest and budgets for graphics. A band's styling on MTV
became the focus for visual marketing.

By the late 1980s dance-floor culture was changing the balance of music-led
entertainment in Britain and reached a critical mass with the explosion of the acid
house movement. The flexible flyer (a portable mini-event poster) was best suited to
promoting the itinerant and semi-spontaneous acid house parties and raves (plate 96).
As the police clamped down on the rave scene in the early 1990s (eventually pushing it
completely underground), flyers could create a clandestine paper trail, passed by hand
like word of mouth, which helped ravers stay one step ahead of the police (plate 95).
Flyers for the illegal raves of the 1990s and early 2000s simply gave a date and a
telephone number so that details could be disseminated at the last minute and the
gathering was harder to stop. Flyer art helped familiarize ravers with the tribal
identities of the different sound systems, and emblems were carried through into
backdrops and wall paintings at the events: intended as new symbols designating the
'free space' of the party (free admission and free from control). Illegal ravers rarely
allowed themselves to be photographed and keeping flyers became a way of
preserving a material memory of the parties.[38]

In the 1990s British design studios such as 8vo and Tomato continued the
tradition of producing exciting graphic design for music events and products. By now,
however, designers were increasingly able to find opportunities for expressive and
experimental work in other fields as a broader range of clients became willing to
embrace challenging graphic design.

Chapter 3 | Into a Digital Age

RENAISSANCE IN OUTDOOR ADVERTISING

Since 2006 people travelling into London on the M4, a main artery into the capital, have been greeted by the JCDecaux Torch – a towering, 32-metre high superstructure that exists to support two giant digital 'poster' screens (plate 97). It is a billboard for the twenty-first century. Shaped like a victory torch and emitting a halo of light, it proudly proclaims the confidence of the outdoor advertising industry. An increase in spending on outdoor advertising that began in the late 1990s has proved to be a continuing trend: it is now the fastest growing traditional form of advertising, with a larger share of the UK advertising market than it has held at any point since the introduction of commercial television.[1] The internet offers advertisers previously undreamed-of opportunities to target specific audiences and quantify the impact of their message. However, since the World Wide Web generates an almost infinite choice of pathways for any individual moving through cyberspace, advertisers who want to intercept a mass audience can look with favour on the fixed geography and more predictable demographics of a physical city. The trump card for a well-placed outdoor poster has always been the fact that it is difficult for the people in a given area to miss – or actively avoid.

Outdoor advertising has been undergoing a form of commercial gentrification. It has always operated alongside a broadly accepted desire to tidy up public space, especially since the 1947 Town and Country Planning Act. The billboard companies, or 'media owners', therefore seek to derive more revenue from fewer, smarter and more targeted poster sites and they are now achieving this more effectively than ever. The outdoor advertising industry has become highly consolidated in Britain, with three main players (JCDecaux, Clear Channel and CBS) competing to win contracts from city councils, rail networks and other landlords to install advertising structures (billboards, bus shelters, and so on) and sell space on them. The size of these companies has accelerated the process of rationalizing poster display through culling

Plate 97
The JCDecaux Torch on the M4
motorway in west London, 2008

Plate 98
HORROR!
Issue 1 of *Scanzine* in situ in
Henry Street, Manchester, 2010

Many designers and artists are
exploring the uses of QR codes.
Scanzine, created by Graeme
Rutherford and Alex Edouard is
a fanzine that passers-by can
scan with their smart phone to
retrieve embedded content. A
single poster provides access to
a selection of illustration, text,
music and video curated around
a particular theme.

less profitable sites and upgrading others – pushing the cost of advertising space to an
ever higher premium. Increasingly, outdoor advertising presents itself as a platform
for 'upscale' brands to address high concentrations of mobile, employed and solvent
consumers, and posters map out the city accordingly. JCDecaux describes its four
flagship towers positioned on roads into London as sitting on the 'wealth corridors'
that connect the capital with the Britain's affluent southern counties.

An ongoing digital makeover is contributing to the changing face of the
industry. The image of down-at-heel billboards of wood, paper and paste is gradually
giving way to high-definition screens and architect-designed street furniture that give
a shiny impression of corporate investment in an environment. Digital technology is
extending the potential of outdoor advertising. Digital screens are considered to be
inherently more eye-catching than their paper counterparts: they emit light, animation
can be used (although generally not roadside), and we have become conditioned to
turn to screens for information and entertainment. The outdoor advertising industry is
starting to lay claim to the best of both worlds – the general impact of the poster
combined with the techniques of quick response and niche marketing associated with
the internet. The ability to change the content of a digital poster display remotely at the
touch of a button allows advertisers to fix their message exactly in time as well as
space. Digital posters can be given a topical, news-flash quality and the programming
of digital sites can be adjusted according to the travel rhythms and behavioural
patterns of the audience. In a somewhat Orwellian development, it is now possible to
embed cameras in posters and link them to facial-recognition software. In this way a
digital billboard will be able to 'read' the gender, age and even the mood of an
approaching consumer and upload an appropriate advertisement.

Accessing the internet is no longer necessarily an indoor or sedentary activity.
Mobile 'smart' phones connected to the internet and GPS (Global Positioning System)
technology encourage an interpenetration of physical space and cyberspace –
allowing outdoor advertising to work seamlessly in conjunction with online activities.
Paper posters now frequently sport Quick Response (QR) codes (pixelated square
barcodes) that can be scanned by a mobile phone to upload hidden content sitting on a
website (plate 98). An advertiser can then prompt the viewer to make an instant online
purchase or provide directions (based on the GPS position of the potential customer)
to the nearest shop that has the product in stock. The poster serves as an internet
bookmark in physical space. 'Augmented Reality' meanwhile works when someone
views a particular point in physical space (such as a poster) through the camera
display on their phone or tablet computer. Digital graphics are triggered which overlay
the scene as it appears on the screen of the device and change in real time as the
viewer shifts position. Used in conjunction with a poster, this technology can make the
products or people featured in a static advertisement appear to spring into life and
start moving and talking.

'Digital posters' and 'digital billboards' are common terms used to describe
the new screen-based formats of outdoor advertising. But how far the concept of a
poster is useful in defining them is a matter of debate. As digital screens slowly start
to replace the footprint of traditional posters in urban space, they noticeably no longer
need to abide by the customary modular dimensions (determined by standard paper
sizes) – a fact that is starting subtly to alter our architectural environment. JCDecaux
names its digital sites in ways that evoke press and television advertising ('glossies',

'double-page spreads', 'widescreen', 'primetime') to impress on their clients that they can match the flexible, targeted nature of those media – that their screens are more than ordinary posters. This suggests the more personalized experience of public space encouraged by digital outdoor advertising. Nevertheless, as large, silent images that compete for the attention of passers-by, these sites do retain some important characteristics of the poster as a mode of communication. For museums concerned with object types and techniques, the problems of collecting and storing digital advertisements and fitting them into a material history of design can contribute to a discontinuity between how we record and understand printed paper forms and their nebulous digital descendants.

Certainly digital advertising enters new creative territory. When the V&A mounted the exhibition *Decode: Digital Design Sensations* in 2009, the curators' aim was to showcase the best of contemporary digital art and design was carried through into the marketing of the exhibition. The museum commissioned leading digital artist Karsten Schmidt to create a digital identity, 'Recode Decode', which was shown on the web and on London Underground's cross track projections (XTPs) (plate 99). Working with generative computer code, Schmidt produced a malleable and ever-changing identity based on a 3D mapping of the wordmark 'DECODE'. Built out of a series of computer operations it was a natively digital piece: a digital concept rather than something simply designed to be displayed on a digital format. Furthermore, the campaign was interactive – an important tenet of digital culture. As the name suggests, 'Recode Decode' was an 'open source' project: Schmidt's code was made freely available on the internet for others to appropriate in creating their own digital artworks, the best of which were fed back onto the XTPs on London Underground. Capturing a weekly audience of twenty million, the XTPs would normally be prohibitively expensive for this kind of project, but were made available through a media partnership between the Museum and CBS (the company that holds the advertising contract on London Underground). When a medium is new there are both commercial and cultural incentives in exploring its creative potential. In the case of 'Recode Decode' the XTPs provided 'the perfect medium to bring art, advertising and digital innovation together'.[2]

BILL POSTERS WILL BE PROSECUTED (BILL POSTERS IS INNOCENT)

The current character of the Web (sometimes described as Web 2.0), exemplified by applications such as Facebook, Twitter, YouTube and Flickr encourages a culture of information sharing, uploading, blogging, leaving feedback, and so on. 'User-generated content' has begun to replace screenfuls of information and graphics created for people to consume passively. And, as noted above, we are developing ever more sophisticated ways of layering digital information over physical space. By contrast, there is increasing intolerance to unauthorized graphic messages and posters being physically uploaded on the street. 'Bill Posters Is Innocent' has been scribbled ubiquitously over notices stating that 'Bill Posters Will Be Prosecuted' since at least the 1960s (although jokes about the persona of 'William Posters' and 'William Stickers' in response to public notices are much older). It is a humorous piece of call-and-answer graffiti supporting the practice of fly-posting and asserting the freedom of the street in defiance of the law. Most fly-posting has always been illegal and there have always been measures taken against it, but in recent years there has been a concerted crackdown. Fly-posting detracts from contemporary narratives of urban regeneration (it often adheres to derelict shops and buildings, drawing attention to urban decay (plate 100) and undermines the contracts between city councils and the big media owners for monopoly rights to advertising space. Many city councils and local authorities proclaim a zero-tolerance policy – assisted by an extended range of legal measures. Perhaps most symbolically fly-posting became an offence under the Antisocial Behaviour Act (2003). In 2004 Camden Council applied for Antisocial Behaviour Orders against Sony, BMG and ambient advertising company, Diabolical Liberties. Tackling antisocial behaviour has become an emotive social theme in Britain in recent years. Discussion of it frequently focuses on fear of the street and the desire to exclude troubling people, noise and graphics. Opponents of fly-posting argue that it distils an essence of criminality into an area and 'can act as an antisocial magnet, encouraging a social downward spiral'.[3] A tendency has developed to visualize the street in terms of crime. Think of the ubiquitous presence of CCTV cameras or the online Police Crime Map launched in 2011: a searchable street-level map of England and Wales that plots recently reported incidences of crime and anti-social behaviour. The idea that fly-posting demarcates problem space could be seen as another manifestation of this.

Councils have stressed the point that multinational music labels are responsible for the majority of illegal fly-posting – companies that could afford mainstream advertising, but choose for reasons of image to make an edgy appearance on the street. While this is true, fly-posting has also been a lifeline for small bands, clubs and theatres. Those who defend fly-posting (including the human rights organization Liberty) point to the danger of editing voices out of public space by making the street an ever more exclusive graphic environment. As graphic design writer Angharad Lewis puts it: 'If you can afford the big, prominent sites you are tolerated and legalised, otherwise, you are deemed beyond control, your message is torn down and you are criminalised'.[4] In the view of Malcolm McLaren (former manager of the Sex Pistols): 'This seems to be about ensuring that control of culture remains with those who can afford it. To ban fly-posting will be another arrow in the heart of our ability as a society to accommodate contrary points of view'.[5]

Threats of legal action have encouraged big brands to move on to other forms of ambient advertising, but fly-posting, especially by local organizations and venues, has not been stamped out. Some city councils have allowed designated fly-posting sites to be set up to provide an affordable legal platform for people to get their message onto the street – although others still consider this an eyesore and an encouragement to fly-post more generally. Some new forms of guerrilla advertising have appeared that touch the city in lighter ways – such as 'clings' (small sheets that adhere to urban surfaces using static which can be removed without trace) or a hand-held projector, developed by British design studio Troika, which can project SMS messages onto walls, windows or the backs of unsuspecting pedestrians. Fly-posting remains a relevant form for both economic and strategic reasons. For people used to viewing material online and having instant access to information, the fly-poster can carry a heightened sense of intrigue – a feeling that there is something happening and something to be discovered. It is a form that does not give everything away at once. For the moment at least, Bill Posters is carrying on the fight.

Plate 100
Fly-posting over a ruined
building in Duke Street,
Liverpool, 2007

RON'S EEL and SHELL FISH

welks, Smoked ~ haddock, Roll mops sea food pieces, kippers, salmon etc...

every Friday and saturday Hoxton st. Market. SHOP LOCAL

Bob and Roberta Smith, Ron's Eel and Shellfish, 2006
A Platform for Art project to coincide with SHOP LOCAL, a project by Bob and Roberta Smith
commissioned by Peer as part of The Shoreditch Festival (www. peeruk.org)
Platform for Art is the art programme for London Underground
Find out more and feedback at tfl.gov.uk/pfa

platform art

MAYOR OF LONDON   Transport for London

THE ART GALLERY OF THE STREETS

Plate 101
RON'S EEL AND SHELLFISH
Bob and Roberta Smith,
commissioned by Platform
for Art (now Art on the
Underground), published by
Transport for London, 2006
Colour offset lithograph
V&A: E.379–2011

One of the ways in which the poster occupies public space today is as public art. The idea of posters forming an 'art gallery of the street' is an old one. Soon after the colour lithographic poster first appeared in Paris in the late nineteenth century, social reformers hailed the possibility for art to ride on the back of advertising out onto the street and into the lives of ordinary people. In the late 1960s and early '70s radical artists created posters as part of a process of redefining the concept of art and situating it outside the gallery. Today public art and site-specific works have an established place in contemporary British art practice. These range from projects sponsored by public or corporate bodies to work stencilled illegally onto the walls of the city by street artists. Contemporary public art frequently ignores the monumental and embraces the ephemeral. Many different sites and artistic media are involved – from performance work on Trafalgar Square's fourth plinth to print works on paper cups. Often it is advertising and propaganda – forms that naturally inhabit the street – which provide a point of departure. In this way artists' posters and billboards appear in public selling no product and demanding no particular action. Instead they make a conceptual intervention in people's daily lives – encouraging them to see the city in a new way.

A key example is Art on the Underground (AoU, previously Platform for Art), a scheme begun by Transport for London in 2000 to install contemporary art across the London Underground network on disused platforms, Oyster card wallets, Tube map covers – and posters. The Underground represents an important historic context for British posters. In the early twentieth century Frank Pick (publicity officer at London Underground and later the managing director) developed a policy of commissioning the best artists and designers of the day to produce posters that would simultaneously promote the Underground's services and enhance people's visual experience of the network. This practice continued until the 1970s, when the Underground engaged in a more hard-selling approach and contracted posters out to advertising agencies. AoU can be seen as a continuation of the Underground's heritage as a patron of art and design – although artistic poster commissions are now conceived of as a separate project to the organization's functional publicity and information.

AoU has used poster commissions to extend installation projects throughout the Underground system and to make links with gallery exhibits and community projects in London. The London Underground is a dense poster environment. AoU posters sit in amongst the general procession of advertising posters in tunnels and escalators. They interrupt the commercial narrative of the space as people suddenly find themselves addressed as something other than consumers or commuters. In some cases the AoU posters are purposefully discordant with the surrounding advertising. 'Ron's Eel and Shellfish', by Bob and Roberta Smith (the double pseudonym used by British artist Patrick Brill) related to the artist's 'Shop Local' project, which had a strong anti-corporate marketing message (plate 101). The artist painted advertising signs for a number of genuine sole traders in the East End of London, reviving a commercial style from the early twentieth century, before the corporate homogenization of the high street, when the individual local trader was a

Plate 102 (below)
Sticker by Sweet Toof, 2010
Digital print in black and
pink on adhesive vinyl
V&A: E.403–2011

A set of teeth and gums is the symbol of British street artist Sweet Toof. In sticker form the motif can be stuck over the mouths of models featured in advertising posters turning them into grinning Sweet Toof characters.

Plate 103 (opposite)
NEVER WORK
Pure Evil, 2008–9
Stencil over a lithographic
poster printed in black and red,
2008–9
V&A: E.378–2011

common figure. As an artistic statement rather than a paid-up advertisement, the eloquently incongruous poster for a small market stall in Hoxton was able to jostle with multi-national advertisers and highlight the imbalance of power represented by modern advertising.

Arguably one of the most popular forms of public art today is Street Art, a form defined by its guerrilla nature: it is placed in public without any selection process or authorization. Street Art methods have their antecedents in spray paint graffiti tagging, but also in political stencils and street poster traditions. The technique of 'paste-ups' borrows from fly-posting: the design is made on thin paper and then pasted onto city surfaces. In this way the work can be prepared in advance in the studio and transferred quickly to the street, reducing the chances of the artist being arrested. Street Art, like the protest posters of the 1970s and '80s can communicate a political message at street level, although this usually flows from a broadly anti-establishment stance rather than an ideological one. In some cases street artists have taken the idea of the propaganda poster as their subject matter. A series of works by British street artist Pure Evil in 2008–9 revisited the political graphics of 1968, taking original Chinese Cultural Revolution posters from that year and stencilling over them with slogans used by French students during the May '68 riots in Paris. He fly-posted these around the East End of London (plate 103). Inevitably, street artists' commentary is sometimes worked over existing posters in situ. Dr.D carries on the tradition of elaborately doctored billboards, while on a smaller scale street art stickers can be swiftly applied to advertising posters, even while travelling down the escalators on London Underground (plate 102).

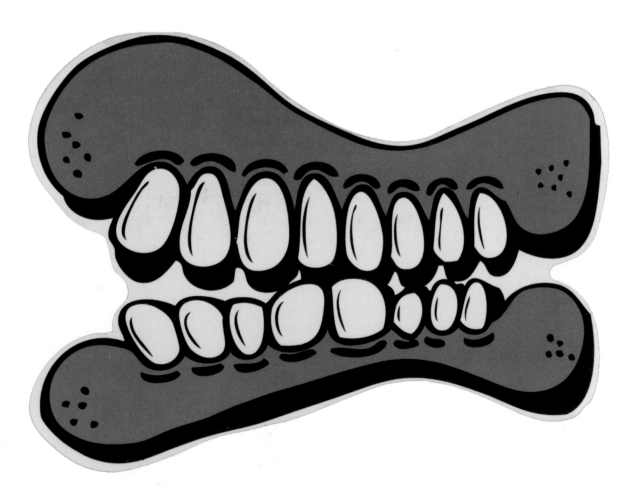

'PEOPLE DO LOVE HUGE PIECES OF PAPER'

Plates 104–107
Four posters from the London
Poster Project, a series of
twenty limited edition posters
commissioned for the London
Design Festival in 2009.
Jonathan Ellery, founder of
Browns; Damon Murray and
Stephen Sorrell, FUEL;
Alan Kitching, The Typographic
Workshop; Andy Altman, Why
Not Associates.
Screenprints in black and red.
V&A: E.382, 398, 397, 385–2011

British graphic designers invariably report a decline in poster commissions over the last ten to fifteen years.[6] Below the radar of big-budget advertisers, it has become harder than ever to convince clients that posters are a viable channel of communication when the same information can be disseminated online through websites, emails and social networking media faster and more cheaply and without the logistics of printing, delivery and display. In 2009 a set of twenty limited edition posters celebrating London were commissioned from leading British graphic designers and studios (plates 104–7) as part of the London Design Festival and exhibited at the V&A during the festival. It was a project that championed the poster as 'one of the oldest and still one of the most powerful communication mediums', as the accompanying text explained. However, the fact that the poster set was a museum-ready enterprise (it came in an archival box set) without a client or definite target audience outside the design community tended instead to highlight the obsolescence of the poster as a practical undertaking in British graphic design.[7]

While their commercial clients have less interest in posters, designers are finding that there is a growing market for self-published posters sold to other designers and the public. Over the last few years a new graphic art scene has emerged

ACID
MOTHERS
TEMPLE
& THE MELTING PARAISO U.F.O

THE ENGINE ROOM
26TH MAY 2010
BRIGHTON · UNITED KINGDOM
LIMITED ED. SERIGRAPHIC POSTER DESIGNED & PRINTED BY RHYSWOOTTON.CO.UK COPYRIGHT TO ARTIST 2010

Plate 108
ACID MOTHERS TEMPLE
Rhys Wootton, 2010
Colour screenprint
V&A: E.83–2011

Rhys Wootton was a founding member of BRAG (the Brighton Rock Art Group, originally named the British Rock Art Group). This collective of around seven members create collectable screenprint posters for bands and tours, selling them at gigs and online. They also hold poster exhibitions.

in Britain that encompasses the work of illustrators, street artists and mainstream graphic designers. As Outline Editions, one of a number of new galleries and websites dedicated to this genre, explains: 'the kind of work which, until recently, only appeared on T-shirts, CD covers and cutting-edge advertising campaigns is now increasingly in demand as affordable wall art'.[8] Graphic art also now has its own annual fair – 'Pick Me Up' at Somerset House. There are significant differences from the domestic poster boom of the late 1960s or the Athena phenomenon of the '70s and '80s. In the '60s people put up posters to identify with popular images or buy into an underground scene. Today there is a more conscious interest in graphic design as a force in contemporary culture: it is savoured for itself. Graphic design critic and author Rick Poynor points to the belief that 'the intense visual pleasures offered by graphic culture are beginning to usurp the place of fine art'.[9]

Since graphic culture is increasingly encountered onscreen, the materiality of graphic wall art assumes greater significance: the difference between accessing an image online and physical possession. As the title 'Pick Me Up' suggests, part of the satisfaction lies in tactility – which often means limited edition screenprints on good quality paper. This has proved to be an outlet for a resurgence in traditional printing techniques. Since the arrival of the Apple Macintosh computer in the 1980s, designers' daily processes have been governed by the interaction of fingertips and screens and operations carried out within the sealed environment of software. In this context the hands-on immediacy and inky alchemy of a traditional printing press can have a peculiar appeal. Evocatively named letterpress studios such as Typoretum or the Society of Revisionist Typographers are reviving the aesthetic of the jobbing playbill printer (centred lettering and mis-matched fonts). South American workshops that mass produce functional street posters on nineteenth-century presses (such as the Lambe Lambe posters in Brazil) have been another recent source of inspiration for British artists and designers.[10] One group of artists has transported all the equipment and contents of an old-fashioned letterpress studio, Carteles la Candelaria in Bogotà, to London for the purpose of making posters. Meanwhile, through organizations such as Poster Roast and BRAG (the Brighton Rock Artist Group), young designers and illustrators are actively developing a screenprint gig poster scene in Britain in response to that currently flourishing in America (plate 108).

Working with pixels on a screen or print on paper are not mutually exclusive processes. Designer Anthony Burrill (often described as the 'godfather of the graphic art scene') contends that the computer is now so well assimilated that it can be treated as one tool among many in a designer's kit. His own work (both commercial and personal) moves effortlessly from his trademark woodblock typographic posters, created with local printers, to experiments with new digital technology. Meanwhile the internet, he suggests, has changed the dynamics of mass distribution since even a small handmade poster project has the latent potential to 'go viral' if uploaded on the web (plates 109–113).

THINK OF YOUR OWN IDEAS

Anthony Burrill

WOR HAR & BE NIC TO PEO

Anthony Burrill

Plates 109–113
Anthony Burrill, five posters
from an ongoing series printed
with Adams of Rye.
Woodblock letterpress on
coloured recycled paper.
V&A: E.407 to 411–2011

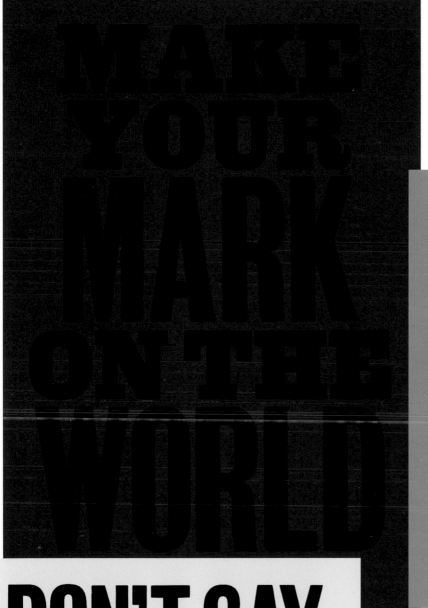

SPEAKING TRUTH TO POWER

In the early twenty-first century events such as the Iraq War and the general election of 2010 have demonstrated that the poster remains an important form of political communication both on the internet and on British streets (plate 114). The invasion of Iraq in 2003 was a moment of reawakening for the protest poster, with many artists and designers turning to the medium as way of expressing their anger and anxiety about the war. Much of this poster activity was located online and several websites were created to provide a dedicated platform for posters on the theme of the war. One of these, Miniature Gigantic, grew out of discussion on a design forum, and described itself as a living online poster exhibition providing a positive outlet for designers' political feelings. It collated international contributions from all sides of the political debate and became an online space where people could share, browse and download designs. The idea of online poster projects inspired by political themes has persisted. Notable recent examples are Designers for Obama (supporting Barack Obama in the 2008 United States presidential election) and Poster4Tomorrow (an international poster competition begun in 2009 that takes a different basic human right for its theme each year). Such enterprises are part campaigning initiatives in their own right and part design exercises to encourage designers to use the poster as a means of political expression. The stated purpose is usually to stimulate debate through poster design. Briefs are broad, and the posters created are not normally tethered to a local campaign or event. They represent the 'collective individualism' and amorphous nature of online political communities, which tend to de-emphasize ideological discourses and tolerate more diverse political identities than geographically convened groups – such as the poster collectives of the 1970s and '80s that were grouped around physical printing presses.

Protest against the Iraq War was also conducted in many countries through mass street demonstrations. In Britain, an anti-war march convened by the Stop the War Coalition In London on 15 February 2003 was the largest ever seen in the UK, with over a million protestors – and many of them carried placards. This was in the mould established by the CND marches of the late 1950s and early '60s: mass direct action aimed at putting pressure on national government policy or at least giving participants the opportunity to register moral dissent from the actions of their government and say 'not in my name'. The Stop the War Coalition followed in the tradition of CND by adopting a strong graphic identity to bind together its actions. This was supplied by the posters/placards designed by David Gentleman: bold words in the clear Helvetica typeface, splattered with red blood. Gentleman is a graphic designer and artist from a generation that remembers the early CND marches to London from the Atomic Weapons Research Establishment at Aldermaston. His initial poster offered to Stop the War simply read 'NO' (plate 115). Gentleman felt that the legibility of placards in press images and news coverage was of primary importance in getting the message across and checked that his designs would work by superimposing thumbnail size versions of them over photographs of previous marches. Printed up as placards and handed out in large numbers to protestors by Stop the War, they created a strong, visible graphic statement reiterated throughout the crowd (plate 116).

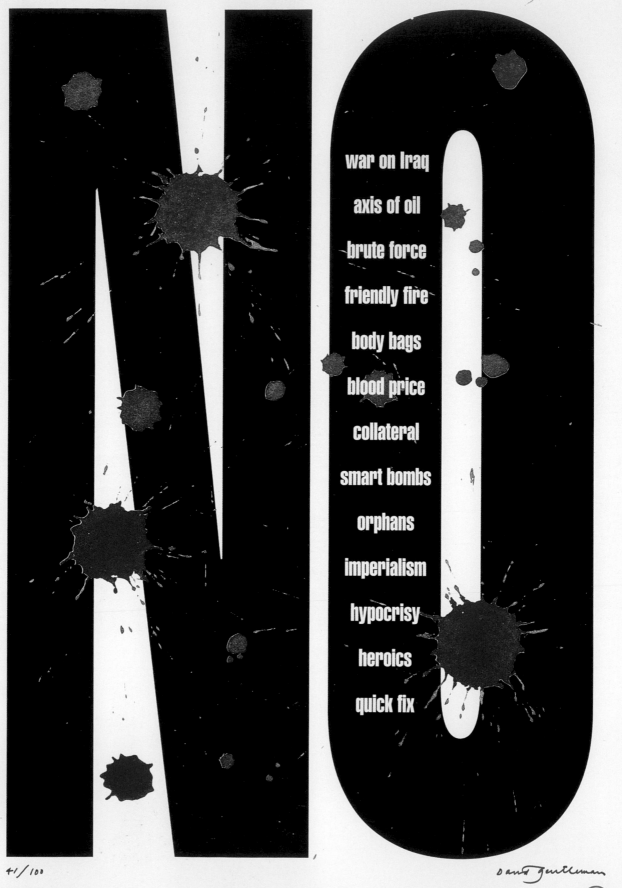

NO

war on Iraq
axis of oil
brute force
friendly fire
body bags
blood price
collateral
smart bombs
orphans
imperialism
hypocrisy
heroics
quick fix

41/100

Stop the War Coalition www.stopwar.org.uk Poster number 3 by David Gentleman 2003

Plate 115 (opposite)
NO
David Gentleman, for the
Stop the War Coalition, 2003
Offset lithograph in black
and red, 2003
V&A: E.1047–2003

This design was mass-produced
as placards by the Stop the
War Coalition and printed in
a limited edition as part of
a portfolio of eight anti-war
posters commissioned from
different artists.

Plate 116 (above)
Protestors marching through
London in a demonstration
against the Iraq War on
15 February 2003

The 'NO' placards designed by
David Gentleman are clearly
visible amongst the avalanche
of protest graphics.

Protests in Britain against government spending cuts in the wake of the 2008 financial crash have so far had a very different graphic character from the Stop the War demonstrations. While the latter fitted into a lineage of graphic design peace posters, much of the paraphernalia carried by the crowd at the national demonstration organized by the Trades Union Congress on 26 March 2011 belonged to the tradition of marching under trade union banners. There were some elaborately embroidered traditional banners, but mostly their modern equivalents – plastic flags and balloons bearing the corporate-style logos and colour schemes of the present- day trade unions. The printed placards distributed to protestors were generally unremarkable and many people made their own with highly personal and sometimes cryptic messages ('Dumbledore wouldn't let this happen', 'Can't afford cheese let alone fees', 'I wish my boyfriend was as dirty as your policies', 'Pint?') scrawled on bits of paper and card. This may have been a result of the disparate agendas of the people campaigning against wide-ranging government cuts. Possibly it was a symptom of the 'Twitter era' – in which people have become used to expressing their personal feelings continuously as 140-character sound bites through instant-messaging social-networking channels. Transposed to the street, it is a style of communication that evades a clear collective message.

The general election of 2010 was predicted to be the first 'e-election', in which online new media would have a significant impact on both campaigning and reporting. This suggested the possibility of the blogosphere intruding into the mainstream media's monopoly on political comment and opinion-leading. It also raised the prospect of tensions between the tightly controlled top-down model of party campaigns (in evidence since the Conservative 1979 campaign) and the more devolved and chaotic nature of online communication. In this context people questioned how the traditional role of the election poster would play out. Labour announced that it was stepping down from billboards altogether, with campaign manager Douglas Alexander stating that 'this election will be won by people, not posters' – that is by word of mouth and online networking.[11] This policy was partly due to an eagerness to engage with new media (inspired by the success of Barack Obama's campaign in 2008), but was mainly determined by the fact that in 2010 Labour lacked the funds for expensive billboard campaigns. Their use of posters was necessarily confined to floating them online, staging a few poster launches for the press, and brief excursions onto poster vans and digital sites.

By contrast the well-funded Conservative Party remained committed to spending on poster space. The poster they launched in January 2010 featuring party leader David Cameron, 'We can't go on like this. I'll cut the deficit, not the NHS', went up on 1000 billboards around the country and quickly became one of the main stories of the election. The initial controversy centred on the odd skin tone of Cameron's face and suspicions that it had been airbrushed or 'photo-shopped'– a process that has come to symbolize the ills of manipulative and hyperreal advertising techniques. In political terms airbrushing provided the Conservatives' opponents with a metaphor for concealment and dissembling. The poster was subjected to brutally direct graffiti on the street (plate 117), but also became an online sensation, with the website mydavidcameron providing a forum for digitally spoofed versions of the poster – even providing a template so that design novices could join in the fun and drop their own slogan into the poster (plate 118). Both Labour and the Liberal Democrats took note

Plate 117
Graffiti over a Conservative
Party election poster in London,
2010

and tried to harness the spirit of digital subversion and mischief. The Liberal Democrats created a spoof party, the 'Labservatives' (meant to highlight a lack of choice between the two main parties) complete with its own logo, websites and posters. Labour meanwhile attempted to 'crowd-source' posters from their supporters by holding a poster competition (Plate 119).

Mydavidcameron seemed to be the signal that the internet was indeed changing the rules for election posters. Some were quick to declare that traditional election posters are now too vulnerable – too easily appropriated and turned into an own goal on the web. In the view of former Conservative politician, Michael Portillo, the message of the David Cameron poster was soon 'lost in ribaldry over the giant images of the leader's face'.[12] However, political online subvertising is largely an activity associated with media savvy, left-leaning cognoscenti. As Chris Burgess points out in an analysis of 2010 poster campaigns, uncommitted voters were still more likely to have seen the original David Cameron poster than the doctored online versions.[13] The Conservatives continued to use billboards throughout the remainder of the election campaign. The 2010 election demonstrated that there was a role for both the traditional party billboard (if you had the funds) and its irreverent online bastards.

In the twenty-first century posters exist on screens and on paper and have a presence in both cyberspace and the physical city. In many cases the cost-effective and instantaneous nature of digital media has superseded the communication function of the traditional printed poster. In Britain in particular there is little patronage from clients to support the poster in the context of graphic design. At the same time the

internet has provided a new platform for self-publishing and distributing poster
designs. Cyberspace and 'real' space provide very different conditions for the poster.
Internet users negotiate posters in new ways. While interactions with physically
encountered posters are generally limited to the extremes of graffiti (destruction) or
collecting (preservation), posters found on the internet can be downloaded, printed
out, forwarded, re-posted on blogs and profile pages, tagged and commented on or
swiftly co-opted and subverted. What gets lost within the fragmented nature of online
communities and the individual interfaces used to access the internet is the traditional
idea of the poster as a public and democratic medium in the sense of collectively
addressing an undifferentiated mass of people. The poster's place in British cities
has always been contested, but many different kinds of contemporary British poster,
from anti-war placards to election billboards and flagship outdoor advertising sites
to pockets of fly-posting, attest to the continued importance of posting messages
in physical space.

Endnotes

INTRODUCTION

1 Alice Twemlow, 'When Did Posters Become Such Wallflowers?', *The Design Observer* http://observatory. designobserver.com/entry.html?entry=5647.
2 Damon Taylor, '*Agit-Pop: Picturing the Revolution in Agit-Pop, 1968–2008, Activist Graphics, Images, Pop Culture*, London Print Studio online catalogue, 2008. http://www.radicalprintshops.org/dokuwiki/lib/exe/fetch. php?media=agitpopcatweb.pdf (accessed 25 July 2011).
3 *Oxford English Dictionary* online

CHAPTER 1

1 'British Poster Designers Know Their Job', *Art and Industry* (1948), vol 44, p.50.
2 Abram Games, 'Approaches to the Poster', *Art and Industry* (1948), vol 45, p. 29.
3 Mass Observation Archive at the University of Sussex, Topic Collection 42: Posters 1936–47, Box 4, 42/4/E: Black Widow poster defacement, 1946.
4 Abram Games, 'The Poster in Modern Advertising', *Journal of the Royal Society of Arts* (April, 1962) vol.cx, no.5069, p.324.
5 Mass Observation Archive, Posters 1936–47.
6 James Fitton quoted on the Museum of London website: http://www.museumoflondon.org.uk/Collections-Research/Research/Your-Research/X20L/objects/record. htm?type=object&id=715401 (accessed 2 July 2011).
7 'London Diary', *New Statesman* (30 November 1946), vol. 32, no.823, pp.393–4.
8 'Posters in the Country', *The Times* (3 September 1946), p. 5.
9 S. John Woods, 'L.P.T.B. Posters' (letter to the editor), *The Times* (16 August 1948), p.5. S. John Woods, who wrote this letter, was responsible for commissioning the celebrated film posters for Ealing Studios in the 1940s and 1950s and was himself a poster designer.
10 'Inquiry into Ban on Advertisements. Trafalgar Square as "National Place"', *The Times* (18 March 1953), p.2.
11 Victoria and Albert Museum, Archive of Art and Design, Sir Hugh Casson, architect, designer, illustrator, journalist: papers 1867–2007, AAD/2008/2/4/1/2.
12 David Gentleman, 'Eckersley, Thomas (1914–1997)', *Oxford Dictionary of National Biography* (Oxford University Press, 2004), online edn, May 2006: http://www.oxforddnb.com/ view/article/66079 (accessed 2 July 2011).
13 Paul Stiff, 'Austerity, Optimism: Modern Typography in Britain after the War' in Paul Stiff (ed.), *Modern Typography in Britain: Graphic Design, Politics and Society* (London: Hyphen Press, 2009), p.9.
14 Ibid.
15 Tom Eckersley, *Poster Design* (London, New York: Studio Publications, 1954), p. 94.
16 Alan Fletcher, Colin Forbes and Bob Gill, *Graphic Design: Visual Comparisons* (London: Studio Books, 1963), p. 5.
17 Alan Brooking, unpublished manuscript.
18 Richard Carr, 'Posters Should Be for People', *Design* (April 1970), vol. 256, p.23.
19 *Hansard*, 'Advertising Industry', House of Commons Debate, 21 November 1958, cols 1503–1620. See col. 1540.
20 Rt Hon. Lord Boothby, 'It's Drab Without the Posters', *The Times* (30 October 1961), p.iii.
21 See the Museum of Neons, Listopada, Poland, and David Crowley, *Warsaw* (London: Reaktion, 2003), pp.124–7.
22 Gordon Cullen, *The Concise Townscape* (London: Architectural Press, 1971; first published 1961).
23 Ernest H. Doubleday, 'Making the Poster Fit the Town', *The Times* (30 October 1961), p.ii.
24 Abram Games, 'The Poster in Modern Advertising', p.325.
25 Virginia Berridge, 'Medicine and the Public: the 1962 Report of the Royal College of Physicians and the New Public Health', *Bulletin of the History of Medicine* (2007), vol. 8, no. 1, p.288.
26 Ibid., p.287.
27 Bill Muirhead, quoted in Alison Fendley, *Saatchi & Saatchi: the Inside Story* (New York: Arcade Publishing, 1996), p.36.
28 '613 More Unemployed Every Day, Mr Prior Complains', *The Times* (23 August 1978), p. 3.
29 Edward Lucie-Smith, *Art in the Seventies* (Oxford: Phaidon, 1980), p.9.
30 Alasdair Reid, 'Outdoor's Golden Opportunity', *Campaign Magazine* (23 July 2004) http://www.campaignlive.co.uk/ news/217513/Outdoor-Ambient-Outdoors-golden-opportunity/?DCMP=ILC-SEARCH (accessed 2 July 2011).
31 London Underground provided display opportunities for cultural institutions and the Tate Gallery displayed advertising posters for other galleries.
32 Hamish Muir quoted in Russell Bestley and Ian Noble, *Up Against the Wall: International Poster Design* (Mies Switzerland, Hove: RotoVision, 2002), p.62.

CHAPTER 2

1 Michael English, cited in Barry Miles, 'At the Edge of Readability: the London Psychedelic School' in Christoph Grunenberg, *Summer of Love: Art of the Psychedelic Era* (London: Tate, 2005), p. 105.
2 Bevis Hillier, *Posters* (New York: Stein & Day, 1969), p. 272.
3 George Melly, 'Poster Power', *Observer Magazine* (3 December 1967), pp.13–17.
4 Bob Borzello, quoted in an untitled article in *The Times* (2 October 1967), p.9.
5 Brian Reade, *Art Nouveau and Alphonse Mucha* (London: HMSO, 1963), p.27.
6 New studies of the poster included Bevis Hillier, *Posters*, John Barnicoat, *A Concise History of Posters* (London, Thames & Hudson, 1972), and Susan Sontag's critical essay 'Posters: Advertisement, Art, Political Artefact, Commodity', in Dugald Stermer, *The Art of Revolution: 96 Posters from Cuba* (London: Pall Mall Press, 1970).
7 Philip Townsend, quoted in Marina Warner, 'The Men Behind the Poster Boom', *Daily Telegraph Magazine* (10 April 1968), p. 34.
8 Christopher Logue, quoted in Davina Lloyd, 'Christopher Logue's Poster Poems', *London Magazine* (1968), vol.8, pp.49–50.
9 Ibid., p.50.
10 Ibid., pp.48–50.
11 See exhibition catalogue *Brighton Festival: Exhibition of Poetry-poster, Organized by Edward Lucie-Smith* (London, Fulham Gallery, 1968).
12 Marina Warner, 'The Men Behind the Poster Boom', p. 34.
13 Susan Sontag, 'Posters: Advertisement, Art, Political Artefact, Commodity', p.xx.
14 Andy Beckett, 'Posters on the Edge', *Independent* (5 January 1996). http://www.independent.co.uk/arts-entertainment/ posters-on-the-edge-1568110.html (accessed 2 July 2011).
15 See John Green, *Ken Sprague – People's Artist* (Stroud, Gloucestershire: Hawthorne Press in partnership with Artery Publications), p. 77.
16 Bevis Hillier, 'A Pioneer of Posters', *The Times* (21 December 1968), p.20.
17 Martin Walker, in *The Hornsey Affair* (by students and staff of Hornsey Art College) (Harmondsworth: Penguin, 1969), p. 74.
18 See http://posterworkshop.co.uk/aboutus.html (accessed 2 July 2011).
19 For a discussion of radical and community printshops in Britain see Jess Baines, 'The Freedom of the Press Belongs to Those Who Control the Press: the Emergence of Radical and Community Printshops in London', in Nico Carpentier et al (eds), *Communicative Approaches to Politics and Ethics in Europe. The Intellectual Work of the 2009 ECREA European Media and Communication Doctoral Summer School* (Tartu, Tartu University Press, 2009), pp.113–28.
20 See John A. Walker, *Left Shift: Radical Art in 1970s Britain* (London: I.B. Tauris, 2002).
21 Dave Fox, 'Poster Film Collective', in Carol Kenna, Lyn Medcalf, Rick Walker (eds), *Printing Is Easy . . .?* (London: Greenwich Mural Workshop, 1986), p.18.
22 Peter Dunn, 'Docklands Community Poster Project', in Carol Kenna et al, *Printing Is Easy . . .?*, p.57.
23 John Berger's television series and publication, *Ways of Seeing* (New York: Viking Press, 1972), was influential in encouraging a social analysis of images.
24 Interview with the author, 2010.
25 'See Red!', *Outwrite* (June 1982), issue 4, p.5.
26 For a discussion of community arts in Britain in the 1970s, see Su Braden, *Artists and People* (London, Henley and Boston: Routledge & Keegan Paul, 1978).
27 John Phillips quoted in Su Braden, *Artists and People*, p.163.
28 See http://www.cspace.org.uk/cspace/archive/docklands/ dock_arch.htm (accessed 2 July 2011).
29 Ibid.
30 Interview with the author, 2010.
31 John A. Walker, *Left Shift*, p. 18.
32 Danny Burns, *Poll Tax Rebellion* (Stirling: AK Press; London: Attack International, 1992), p. 67.
33 George Melly, 'Poster Power', p.13.
34 Jamie Reid, the graphic designer responsible for the 'cut and paste' aesthetic of punk band the Sex Pistols had previously been involved with the community arts movement through the Suburban Press.
35 For Rock Against Racism see David Widgery, *Beating Time* (London: Chatto & Windus, 1986).
36 Malcolm Garrett, quoted in Kevin Edge, *The Art of Selling Songs: Graphics for the Music Business, 1690–1990* (London: Futures Publications, 1991), p.96.
37 'Overload and Heaven Sent, an interview with Martin Hannett, 1989', *Vagabond*, issue 1, 1991.
38 One of the few photographers who did record the rave scene was Molly Macindoe. See Molly Macindoe, *Out of Order: a Photographic Celebration of the Free Party Scene* (Bristol: Tangent Books, 2011).

CHAPTER 3

1 Reid, 'Outdoor's Golden Opportunity'.
2 Jane Rosier, quoted in Sky Arts report, *Building Innovative Arts Partnerships*, p.17, www.skyarts.co.uk/images/uploads/ SkyArtsBuildingInnovativeArtsPartnershipsReport.pdf (accessed 27 June 2011).
3 *Coventry City Council Fly-posting Policy Consultation*, 1.3.3, kb.keepbritaintidy.org/flyposting/publications/consult.pdf (accessed 27 June 2011).
4 Malcolm Frost, Angharad Lewis and Aidan Winterburn (eds), *Street Talk: the Rise and Fall of the Poster* (Mulgrave: Images Publishing, 2006), p.32.
5 Malcolm McLaren, quoted in Hugh Muir, 'Writing's on the Wall for Flyposting', *Guardian* (18 September 2004).
6 Section heading is a quote from Michael Johnson, 'What Next for Poster Design?' in Johnson Banks, *Thought for the Week* (blog), 18 March 2010. http://www.johnsonbanks.co.uk/thoughtfortheweek/index. php?thoughtid=552 (accessed 5 July 2011).
7 See Rick Poynor 'All Mouth and Trousers? London Designers Show How Little They Care for the Poster Form', *Eye Blog* (17 January 2010), blog.eyemagazine.com/?p=448 (accessed 27 June 2011).
8 Outline Editions website www.outline-editions.co.uk/about (accessed 27 June 2011).
9 Rick Poynor, 'The Graphic Grab', *Guardian* (28 August 2004).
10 See for example 'Lambe Lambe', *Creative Review*, (January 2009), or the video of street artist Pure Evil working with Grafika Fidalga Studio in São Paulo, Brazil http://www.youtube.com/watch?v=9grucvvl2dg (accessed 25 July 2011).
11 Douglas Alexander, quoted by Chris Burgess, Dominic Wring, Roger Mortimore and Simon Atkinson (eds), *Political Communication in Britain. The Leader Debates, the Campaign and the Media in the 2010 General Election* (Houndmills, Basingstoke: Palgrave, 2011), p.190.
12 Michael Portillo, 'Tories Are Hurting the Most in the Crisis', *Sunday Times* (2 February 2010).
13 Burgess et al (eds), *Political Communication in Britain*, p.185.

Acknowledgements

I would like to thank the many people who have provided expert guidance and shared information with me in the course of writing this book. These include Tom Adams, Jenna Andreotti, Mike Baker, Natalie Bates, Len Breen, Alan Brooking, Anthony Burrill, Emma Clackson, David Dawson, Peter Dunn, Kevin Edge, Charley Uzzell Edwards, David Elliott, Ruth Gregory, Leo Griffin, Christine Halsall, Richard Hollis, Michael Johnson, Ed Jones, Carol Kenna, Peter Kennard, David King, Steve Lobb, Molly Macindoe, Suzy Mackie, Dave McEvoy, Alex Maranzano, Jonathan Miles, Vaughan Oliver, Cat Picton Phillipps, John Phillips, Paul Rennie, Bronwen Rice, Jo Robinson, Cathy Ross, Syd Shelton, Pru Stevenson, Chris Thomas, Philip Townsend, Derek Walker, Martin Walker, Jeff Willis, Melanie Wilson, Sarah Wilson, Rhys Wootton and the members of BRAG, Jon Wozencroft.

Many of the posters that appear in this book have generously been donated to the V&A. Amongst these are posters from the Schreyer Collection, the gift of Leslie, Judith and Gabri Schreyer and Alice Schreyer Batko through the American Friends of the V&A. Also represented are recent donations from BRAG, Anthony Burrill, Greenwich Mural Workshop, Peter Kennard and Cat Picton Phillipps, Minale Tattersfield Design Strategy, Suzy Mackie and Pru Stevenson (founder members of the See Red Women's Workshop) and Bronwen Rice (daughter of Julia Franco, founder member of the See Red Women's Workshop). My thanks go to all those who have supplied images and allowed posters in their collections to be reproduced.

Huge thanks are due to the following colleagues at the V&A: Christopher Breward, Lily Crowther, Liz Miller, Ella Ravilious, Gill Saunders, Louise Shannon, Margaret Timmers, Ghislaine Wood, the Prints Section and the V&A Photo Studio. For the production of the book I would like to thank Lewis Ronald for photography, Anjali Bulley and Kate Phillimore of V&A Publishing, Liz Cowen for copyediting and Will Web for design. I would also like to gratefully acknowledge the support and encouragement I have received from Maureen Flood, Louise Hull, Laura Janes, Danny Lang and Alison Rosenblitt.

With special thanks to the late John J. F. Flood

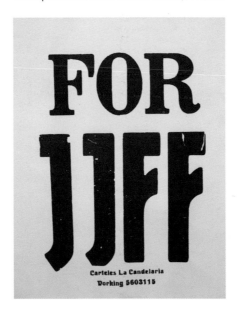

Further Reading

Jess Baines, 'The Freedom of the Press Belongs to Those Who Control the Press: the Emergence of Radical and Community Printshops in London' in Nico Carpentier et al (eds), *Communicative Approaches to Politics and Ethics in Europe. The Intellectual Work of the 2009 ECREA European Media and Communication Doctoral Summer School* (Tartu, Tartu University Press, 2009)

David Bernstein, *Advertising Outdoors: Watch This Space!* (London: Phaidon, 1997)

Julia Bigham, 'Day-Glo Mind Blow', *Eye Magazine*, vol.42

Su Braden, *Artists and People* (London, Henley and Boston: Routledge & Keegan Paul, 1978)

Kevin Edge, *The Art of Selling Songs: Graphics for the Music Business, 1690–1990* (London: Futures Publications, 1991)

Malcolm Frost, Angharad Lewis and Aidan Winterburn (eds), *Street Talk: the Rise and Fall of the Poster* (Mulgrave: Images Publishing, 2006)

Abram Games, 'Approaches to the Poster', *Art and Industry* (1948), vol.45

Richard Hollis, *Graphic Design: a Concise History* (London: Thames & Hudson, 1994)

Carol Kenna, Lyn Medcalf, Rick Walker (eds), *Printing Is Easy . . .?* (London: Greenwich Mural Workshop, 1986)

Adam Lent, *Social Movements in Britain since 1945* (Basingstoke: Palgrave, 2001)

Liz McQuiston, *Graphic Agitation: Social and Political Graphics since the Sixties* (London: Phaidon, 1993)

Liz McQuiston, *Graphic Agitation, 2: Social and Political Graphics in the Digital Age* (London, 2004)

Liz McQuiston, *From Suffragettes to She Devils: Women's Liberation and Beyond* (London: Phaidon, 1997)

George Melly, 'Poster Power', *Observer Magazine* (3 December 1967)

Barry Miles, 'At the Edge of Readability: the London Psychedelic School' in Christoph Grunenberg, *Summer of Love: Art of the Psychedelic Era* (London: Tate, 2005)

Toby Mott, Susanna Greeves and Simon Ford, *Loud Flash: British Punk on Paper* (London: Haunch of Venison, 2010)

Rick Poynor, *Communicate: Independent British Graphic Design since the Sixties* (London: Laurence King, 2005)

Paul Rennie, *Modern British Posters, Art Design and Communication* (London: Black Dog Publishing, c.2010)

Margaret Timmers (ed.), *The Power of the Poster* (London: V&A Publications, 1998)

Alice Twemlow, 'When Did Posters Become Such Wallflowers?', *Design Observer* http://observatory.designobserver.com/entry. html?entry=5647

John A. Walker, *Left Shift: Radical Art in 1970s Britain* (London, New York: I.B. Tauris Publishers, 2002)

Marina Warner, 'The Men Behind the Poster Boom', *Daily Telegraph Magazine* (10 April 1968)

Index

Page numbers in *italic* refer to the illustrations

Picture Credits

Images and copyright clearance have been kindly supplied as listed below. Unless otherwise stated, images are © V&A Images.

Courtesy of the Victoria and Albert Museum/Gift of the American Friends of the V&A; Gift to the American Friends by Leslie, Judith and Gabri Schreyer and Alice Schreyer Batko, 14, 16, 31, 52, 68, 72, 85

Courtesy of Andy Altman, 109 right

Photo by Nick Ansell/PA Archive/
Press Association Images, 121

Courtesy of the Archive of Modern Conflict, 60

© Association of Members of Hornsey College of Art, 62, cover

© David Bailey, 82

Courtesy of Andy Barefoot, 120 top left, cover

Courtesy of Natalie Bates, 95

Brendan Beirne/Rex Features, 9

© Peter Blake. All rights reserved, DACS 2011, 53

Courtesy of Len Breen, 67

Courtesy of Alan Brooking, 31

Courtesy of Martin Brown, 106

Courtesy of Robin Brown, 120 bottom left

Courtesy of Anthony Burrill, 112-3

Courtesy of Sara Cohen, The Institute of Popular Music, University of Liverpool, 103

Courtesy of David Collins, 83

Photo by The Conservative Party Archive/
Getty Images, 32, 35

© Theo Crosby Estate / Whitechapel Gallery, Whitechapel Gallery Archive, 46

Crown Copyright 7, 15, 17, 25

Courtesy of Pen Dalton, 72, cover

Design Council Slide Collection at Manchester Metropolitan University, 29

© The Designers Republic, 45

Courtesy of Peter Dunn and Loraine Leeson, 75

Courtesy of Jonathan Ellery, Founder of Browns, 108

© Estate of Michael English, 84, cover

© The Financial Times Ltd (2012),
All Rights Reserved, 23

Friends of the Earth (England, Wales & N. Ireland) www.foe.co.uk, 83

© By permission of Judy and Tim Fitton, 19

Courtesy of Fletcher Studio, 28

Courtesy of Chris Fox, 120 centre left

Photo by Fox Photos/Getty Images, 21

Courtesy of FUEL, 109 left

© Gallaher Ltd, 36, cover

Estate of Abram Games, 14

Courtesy of Ken Garland, 61

Courtesy of Peter Gatley (Art Director),
John Pallant (Writer), BMP (Agency), 33

Courtesy of David Gentleman, 44, 116

Photo by Getty Images, 37

© Stephen Gill, 8, back cover

Courtesy of Hales Gallery and the Artist, 104

© Richard Hamilton. All Rights Reserved, DACS 2011/
Whitechapel Gallery, Whitechapel Gallery Archive, 46

Courtesy of Michael Hanley, 120 top right

Photo by Bert Hardy/Picture Post/Getty Images, 20

Courtesy of Alex Harrowell/www.harrowell.org.uk,
120 second from top left

© Nigel Henderson Estate/Whitechapel Gallery,
Whitechapel Gallery Archive, 46

Estate of FHK Henrion, 23

© Richard Hollis and Modern Art Oxford, 42

Courtesy of Jack Hurley, 120 middle right

Courtesy of JCDecaux, 96

© Johnson Banks/The British Council, 43

Courtesy of Carol Kenna, Greenwich Mural
Workshop, 73

Courtesy of Peter Kennard, 80, 81

Courtesy of kennardphillipps, 114, cover

Courtesy of David King, 77, 78, cover

Courtesy of Alan Kitching, 109 centre

Photo by Dan Kitwood/Getty Images, 119

By Christopher Logue, copyright © Christopher Logue,
1969, 54, cover

Copyright London Underground/Transport for
London 2010, 10

Photo by Peter MacDiarmid/REUTERS, 117

Courtesy of Suzy Mackie and Pru Setevenson (founder
members of the See Red Women's Workshop) and
Bronwen Rice (daughter of Julia Franco, founder
member of the See Red Women's Workshop), 70, 71

Courtesy of John Maybury, 11

Courtesy of Mike McInnerney, 49

Courtesy of Minale Tattersfield & Partners Ltd., 40

© John Morris (design & text), Paul Trevor

(photograph), 34

Courtesy of Hamish Muir and Mark Holt, 92

© Museum of London, 12

Courtesy of MyDavidCameron, 120 second from top
right; second from bottom right; bottom right

© National Theatre, 41

© Nike, 39

Courtesy of Graeme Norways (Art Director),
Nick Hazzard (Copywriter), Lester Bookbinder
(Photographer), 36

Courtesy of Vaughan Oliver, 7, 93, cover

© Trustees of the Paolozzi Foundation, Licensed
by DACS 2011, 48

Courtesy of John Pasche, 85

Courtesy of John Phillips at London Print Studio, 73

Courtesy of the Piech Archive, 76

Poster by Jan Pieńkowski for Gallery Five, 57

© John Piper Estate, 22

© Playtex UK Ltd, 38, cover

Courtesy of The Poster Collective, 68, 69

Courtesy of David and John Prescott, 120
second from bottom left

© Pure Evil, 107

Jamie Reid, courtesy Isis Gallery, 89, cover

© Spencer Rowell, 58

© Royal Mail Group Ltd 2011, courtesy of The British
Postal Museum & Archive, 52, cover

© Royal Society for the Prevention of Accidents, 16

Courtesy of Peter Saville Studio, 93

Courtesy of Scanzine, 99

© Karsten Schmidt, 101

Martin Sharp/All Rights Reserved, DACS 2011,
50, cover

Courtesy of Syd Shelton and Ruth Gregory, 91

© TFL from the London Transport Museum
collection, 18

Paul Trevor © 2012, 79

© V&A images, 21

Courtesy of Gee Vaucher, 90

Courtesy of Martin Walker and Bernadette Britain, 64

© Patrick Ward / supplied by Guardian News and
Media Ltd., 51

Courtesy of Nigel Weymouth and the Estate of
Michael English, 49

Courtesy of Melanie Wilson, 94

Courtesy of Sarah Wilson, 63

© Rhys Wootton/Octopus Gallery, 110